Preface

This collection of classroom activities is designed to add both variety and interest to 'A' level Computing courses. The emphasis is very much on student involvement and "active learning" and the activities are intended to complement, not replace, more traditional methods of teaching and learning.

For most of the activities, students should work in small groups. Some tasks, such as the **matching exercises** and **quick quizzes**, are useful ways of starting a lesson or of reviewing a lesson at its close. Others, such as the **crosswords** and **dominoes**, add variety to revision sessions. The activities help to extend students' knowledge and understanding by getting them to *process* information rather than just *reproduce* it.

For each type of activity, there is an introductory page explaining its purpose and setting out the way in which it can be run, followed by a set of exercises. Answers are given at the back of the book. The later exercises in each of the main sections tend to be more challenging. Apart from the quick quizzes, the exercises are designed to be photocopied and distributed to students. They can also be loaded onto an intranet.

The list of contents gives an overview of the range of activities covered in this book. To locate an exercise on a given topic, see the index at the back. Supporting software for exercises 28, 65 and 68 to 72 can be downloaded from the publisher's website www.payne-gallway.co.uk

Contents

Siobahn

Classroom Activities
for
'A' Level Computing

Ian Flynn

Acknowledgements

Cover illustration © Richard Chasemore 2004

Cover design by Direction123.com

1st edition 2004

10 09 08 07 06
10 9 8 7 6 5 4

10-digit ISBN: 1 904467 72 5
13-digit ISBN: 978 1 904467 72 4

Copyright © 2004 Ian Flynn

Disclaimer

The author has made every effort to ensure the accuracy of the material. The author and the publisher will not accept liability for any loss or damages arising from the information contained in this material.

Printed in Great Britain by

Pear Tree Press Ltd, Stevenage Herts, England

Matching Exercises

For these exercises, you give students two lists and ask them to pair up items from each list.

These exercises are useful as quick review sessions at the beginning or end of a lesson. They have two advantages over Question & Answer sessions:

- it is easier to involve every student;
- students are required to show some *understanding* of the topic, not just *reproduce information*.

Delivery

1. Divide the class into pairs or threes, and give each student a copy of the worksheet.
2. Ask each group to pair up items and to agree an order. Emphasise that they *must* reach agreement.
3. Review the activity with the whole class, and reach final agreement.

Since students have to justify their choices to the rest of the group, discussion is the most valuable part of the activity. In some exercises an element of ambiguity has been built in to stimulate this discussion.

Timing

These exercises take around ten minutes. Allow more time if you plan to have a follow-up discussion.

Exercise 1   Matching Basic Hardware Components

Match each task on the right with the most appropriate hardware component on the left. You are expected to use each component exactly once, so decide on the best combination.

When you have agreed your answers, write the appropriate number alongside each hardware component.

Hardware component		Task	
A	Processor	1	Transmitting data between components
B	Input device	2	Carrying out program instructions
C	Output device	3	Entering data
D	System bus	4	Storing a program that is running
E	Main Memory	5	Storing a program that will be run later
F	Secondary or backing store	6	Displaying results

Exercise 2   Matching Application Software

A business has several application software packages and several tasks that need to be carried out. Match each task on the right with the most suitable type of application software on the left. Although some software could be used for more than one of the tasks, you are expected to use each type of software exactly once, so decide on the best combination.

When you have agreed your answers, write the appropriate number alongside each type of software.

Application software type		Task	
A	Word processor	1	Storing customer records
B	Spreadsheet	2	Designing a new product
C	Presentation graphics package	3	Creating a glossy catalogue of products
D	Desktop publishing program	4	Preparing a sales report for the Board of Directors
E	Database	5	Creating a customer invoice
F	CAD program	6	Producing a letter

Exercise 3   Matching Storage Media

Match each task on the right with the most appropriate storage medium on the left.

When you have agreed your answers, write the appropriate number alongside each storage medium.

Storage medium		Task	
A	Memory stick	1	Holding programs frequently used on a computer
B	CD-ROM	2	Archiving 300 Mb of data
C	Floppy disk	3	Backing up an 80 Gb network server disk
D	Magnetic DAT tape	4	Distributing a 500 Mb electronic encyclopaedia
E	CD-R	5	Storing high resolution digital photographs
F	Hard disk	6	Transferring a 100K file between two standalone desktop computers

Exercise 4   Matching Data Representation 1

Match each use on the right with the most suitable data representation on the left. You are expected to use each representation exactly once, so decide on the best combination.

When you have agreed your answers, write the appropriate number alongside each form of data representation.

Representation		Use	
A	Pure Binary	1	Photographs
B	ASCII	2	Numbers shown on a calculator display
C	Bit mapping	3	Chinese characters
D	BCD	4	UK car registration numbers
E	Unicode	5	Building plans
F	Vector mapping	6	Exam marks

Exercise 5   Matching Data Representation 2

Match each use on the right with the most likely form of data representation on the left. You are expected to use each representation exactly once, so decide on the best combination.

When you have agreed your answers, write the appropriate number alongside each form of data representation.

[Hint: start with the ones you are sure of, and then consider the best way of allocating the others.]

Representation		Use	
A	2s complement integer	1	A phone number stored in a database
B	ASCII	2	A phone number being displayed on a mobile phone while being dialled
C	Boolean	3	The price of a music CD
D	BCD	4	A student's test score
E	Floating point number	5	A person's gender
F	Fixed point number	6	A temperature reading

Exercise 6　Matching Data Validation

Match each data item on the right with the most suitable validation check on the left. You are expected to use each type of validation exactly once, so decide on the best combination.

When you have agreed your answers, write the appropriate number alongside each type of validation check.

Validation check		Data item	
A	Range check	1	The existence of an item in stock
B	Check digit	2	A new-style car registration number
C	File lookup	3	Week number
D	Picture / format check	4	Product code
E	Character count	5	Account number
F	Hash total	6	An ISBN

Exercise 7   Matching Data Structures 1

Match each task on the right with the most appropriate data structure on the left. Match each task once. **Note that there are more tasks than data structures, so you will need to use some of the data structures more than once.**

When you have agreed your answers, write the appropriate number(s) alongside each data structure.

Data structure	Task
A Queue	1 Reversing the items in a list
B Stack	2 Rapid retrieval of one item of data
C Tree	3 Storing characters in a printer buffer
	4 Sorting a list of words into alphabetical order
	5 Storing jobs waiting to be printed on a shared network printer

Exercise 8   Matching Data Structures 2

Match each task on the right with the most suitable data structure on the left. You are expected to use each data structure exactly once, so decide on the best combination.

When you have agreed your answers, write the appropriate number alongside each data structure.

Data structure		Task	
A	Queue	1	Storing return addresses when procedures are called
B	Array	2	Storing characters typed at the keyboard
C	Stack	3	Organising data in non-contiguous memory blocks
D	Tree	4	Storing data that needs to be accessed directly
E	Linked List	5	Converting expressions between infix and postfix notation

Exercise 9   Matching Human Computer Interfaces

Match each task on the right with the most likely means of user interaction on the left. You are expected to use each means of user interaction exactly once, so decide on the best combination.

When you have agreed your answers, write the appropriate number alongside each means of user interaction.

Means of user interaction	Task / Use
A Graphical user interface	1 A basic operating system
B Command line interface	2 Desktop publishing
C Menu interface	3 Entering data into a database
D Voice recognition	4 A machine to be used by a blind person
E Form dialogue	5 A personal organiser
F Stylus	6 A "help" system

Exercise 10 Matching Systems Development

Match each term on the right with a different development phase on the left. You are expected to use each item exactly once, so decide on the best combination.

When you have agreed your answers, write the appropriate number alongside each development phase.

Development phase		Term	
A	Analysis	1	Unit testing
B	Design	2	Usability
C	Development	3	Volumetrics
D	Implementation	4	Adaptation
E	Evaluation	5	File conversion
F	Maintenance	6	Hardware specification

Exercise 11   Matching Legislation

Match each piece of legislation on the right with the activities on the left. You will need to use each piece of legislation more than once.

When you have agreed your answers, write the appropriate number alongside each activity.

Activity		Legislation	
A	Unauthorised access to a computer system	1	Data Protection Act
B	Storing personal data	2	Computer Misuse Act
C	Restrictions on data being sent abroad	3	Copyright Designs and Patents Act
D	Creating and releasing computer viruses		
E	Copying software		
F	Using someone else's code in your own program		
G	Keeping information accurate and up to date		
H	Making unauthorised changes to data on someone else's computer		

Exercise 12   Matching CPU Components

Match the description on the left with the most suitable CPU component on the right. You are expected to use each component exactly once, so decide on the best combination.

When you have agreed your answers, write the appropriate number alongside each description.

Description		Component	
A	Decodes instructions	1	Clock
B	Holds the current instruction	2	ALU
C	Holds the address of the next instruction	3	CU
D	Carries out arithmetic operations	4	CIR
E	Synchronises operations	5	Accumulator
F	Holds results of arithmetic operations	6	PC

Exercise 13 Matching Addressing Modes

Match the tasks on the left with the most suitable addressing mode on the right. You are expected to use each mode exactly once, so decide on the best combination.

When you have agreed your answers, write the appropriate number alongside each task.

Task		Addressing mode	
A	Initialise a counter	1	Direct
B	Jump forward ten places	2	Indexed
C	Process the elements of an array	3	Indirect
D	Access the fullest possible range of memory locations	4	Immediate
E	Gain efficient access to a limited range of memory locations	5	Relative

Exercise 14   Matching Operating System Concepts

Match each operating system function on the left with the most appropriate concept on the right. You are expected to use each concept exactly once, so decide on the best combination.

When you have agreed your answers, write the appropriate number alongside each function.

OS function		Concept	
A	Memory management	1	Addressable blocks
B	I/O management	2	Access control
C	User interface	3	Code sharing
D	File management	4	Scheduling
E	Task management	5	Handlers and drivers
F	System security	6	Job control language

Exercise 15 Matching Operating System Terms

Match each term on the left with the most suitable description on the right. You are expected to use each description exactly once, so decide on the best combination.

When you have agreed your answers, write the appropriate number alongside each term.

Term			Description
A	Process	1	A fixed size block of memory
B	Virtual memory	2	The movement of blocked processes to backing store and runnable processes to main memory
C	Page	3	Late-binding code that can be shared between processes
D	Thread	4	A program for which execution has started
E	Swapping	5	Part of a process that can run in parallel with other parts
F	DLL	6	A section of hard disk used as an extension to main memory

Exercise 16   Matching Programming Languages

Match each task on the right with the most suitable programming language on the left. You must use each language exactly once, so decide which is the best combination.

When you have agreed your answers, write the appropriate number alongside each language.

Language		Task	
A	Assembly language	1	Solving a set of complex mathematical equations
B	Java	2	Managing simultaneous processes
C	Prolog	3	Creating an Internet-based system
D	Ada	4	Handling large data files
E	Cobol	5	Creating an expert system
F	Fortran	6	Writing time-critical components of an operating system

Exercise 17 Matching LAN Components

Match each task on the right with the most appropriate LAN component on the left. You are expected to use each component exactly once, so decide on the best combination.

When you have agreed your answers, write the appropriate number alongside each component.

LAN component		Task	
A	Network interface card	1	Distributing signals received on one communication link to all other links
B	Server	2	Linking the LAN to the Internet
C	Switch	3	Connecting two LANs of the same type
D	Router	4	Holding a shared database
E	Hub	5	Forwarding data packets onto the appropriate path to reach their destination
F	Bridge	6	Linking a device to the network cable

Exercise 18 Matching Internet Security

Match each security hazard on the right with the most appropriate security method on the left.

When you have agreed your answers, write the appropriate number alongside each security method.

Security method		Hazard	
A	Firewall	1	Unauthorised access to an individual's webmail service
B	Encryption	2	Viruses in downloaded message attachments
C	Anti-virus software	3	Fraudulent collection of bank account data by someone using a false identity
D	Digital certificate	4	Unauthorised interception of messages
E	CLI (caller line identification)	5	Unauthorised remote access to a computer
F	Password	6	Unauthorised use of a home user's ISP dial-up account

Exercise 19   Matching Internet Services

Match each task on the right with the most appropriate service or utility on the left.

When you have agreed your answers, write the appropriate number alongside each service / utility.

Service / Utility		Task	
A	IRC	1	Managing a remote web site
B	A browser	2	Creating a dynamic web page
C	A Telnet utility	3	Accessing specialist news groups
D	Usenet	4	Exchanging chat messages
E	ASP	5	Transferring files
F	An FTP utility	6	Reading web pages

Exercise 20 Matching Assembly Language

Suppose a particular processor uses 16-bit addresses, a 16-bit word size and a number of 16-bit registers labelled R0, R1, etc. Some assembly language instructions for this processor are given below. Match each instruction on the right with the most appropriate task on the left. Each instruction should be assigned to exactly one task.

When you have agreed your answers, write the appropriate number alongside each task.

Task		Instruction	
A	Store the result of an operation in a specific memory location	1	JMP FFFF
B	Go back to previous instruction	2	AND R1 FF00
C	Add the contents of a specific memory cell to the contents of a register	3	ST R1 0020
D	Divide the contents of a register by 4	4	SAR R1 2
E	Mask out half the bits in a register	5	ADD R1 #2
F	Increment a register by 2	6	ADD R1 0400

Ordering Exercises

In these exercises, students have to agree an order for a list of items, such as storage devices or forms of file organisation, according to at least two different criteria. You can use these exercises as quick review sessions at the beginning or end of a lesson, or to trigger further discussion (since that the students are likely to have ordered items differently for different tasks).

As with the *matching* exercises, discussion between students is the most educationally valuable part of the activity.

Delivery

1   Divide the class into pairs or threes and give each student a copy of the worksheet.

2   Ask each group to agree an order for each task on the sheet. Emphasise that they must reach agreement.

3   Review the activity with the whole class and reach final agreement.

4   Optionally, the exercise can be used as the starting point for further discussion, using such questions as "Is there a best form of file organisation?" or "Why do we have several different types of secondary storage?"

Timing

Allow ten to fifteen minutes.

Exercise 21 Ordering Storage Media

Work with your group to consider the following five storage media:

- CD-RW
- DVD-RW
- memory stick
- hard disk drive
- floppy disk
- RAM

Task 1   Arrange the storage media in order of storage capacity, largest first.

(largest) _____

　　　　　 _____

　　　　　 _____

　　　　　 _____

　　　　　 _____

(smallest) _____

Task 2   Arrange the storage media in order of access speed, fastest first.

(fastest) _____

　　　　　 _____

　　　　　 _____

　　　　　 _____

　　　　　 _____

(slowest) _____

Exercise 22   File Organisation

A mail-order company stores several thousand customer records in a data file. Together with your group, consider four types of file organisation that might be used:

- Sequential File
- Indexed File
- Serial file
- Random Access / Hash File

Task 1   Arrange the four types of file organisation in order, according to the average time it takes to <u>add</u> a record to the file, fastest first.

(fastest) _____

_____

_____

(slowest) _____

Task 2   Arrange the four types of file organisation in order, according to the average time it takes to <u>retrieve</u> a record from the file using its primary key, fastest first.

(fastest) _____

_____

_____

(slowest) _____

Dominoes

This activity is based on an idea quoted in "Active Whole-Class Teaching" by Robert Powell (www.robertpowellpublications.com), a mine of good ideas. He gives a Chemistry example, but the idea seems applicable to a wide range of subjects and certainly works for Computing. Each of the next four pages carries a template for a set of dominoes on a different area of Computing.

Preparation before the lesson

1   Decide how many groups there will be and make one copy of the sheet of dominoes per group on differently coloured paper or card. Card will last longer, but paper will do. It is important that the sets are different colours so that they can be stored and reused easily.

2   Cut each sheet along the thick lines to form a set of 18 dominoes.

Delivery

1   Organise students into groups of three or four around separate tables and give each group a set of dominoes.

2   One player in each group deals the dominoes.

3   Players take it in turn to place a domino on the table, forming a chain as in conventional dominoes.

4   To place a piece, a player must give a connection between the word (or phrase) on the end of the domino on the table and the word being placed next to it. For example, a player placing *main memory* next to *software* may say "for software to run it must be loaded into main memory".

| Spread-sheet | Backing Store | CD-ROM | Software | | Main Memory | Input Device |

5   Other players may challenge if they do not agree that the connection is valid; the teacher acts as referee. If a player is successfully challenged, or cannot go, that player misses a turn.

6   If players are having difficulty they can be allowed to join dominoes to a point in the middle of the chain rather than the end, though this is not usually necessary.

7   The "winner" is the first player to place all her/his dominoes on the table.

8   If the activity is going well then further rounds can be played, either between the same players or with players moving between tables.

A variation that works well is to have three pairs of partners playing together at each table. This leads to interaction on different levels and teamwork as well as competition.

Timing

Allow anything from 15 minutes upwards, depending how many rounds are played.

Exercise 23 Basic hardware and software

Hardware	Bit-mapped	CD-RW Drive	Resolution
Input Device	Main Memory	CD-ROM	Software
Magnetic Disk Drive	Program	Storage Medium	LCD
Spreadsheet	Backing Store	Word Processor	Floppy Disk
Processor	Utilities	Bar Code Reader	Operating System
Application Software	Printer	Output Device	Keyboard
System Software	Instructions	Generic Software	Data Bus
Data	Graphics Card	Mouse	Optical Disk
VDU	DTP	Image	Laptop Computer

Exercise 24 Systems Analysis

Information	DFD	Interview	Client
Analyst	Objectives	Observation	Data
Procedures	Manager	Questionnaire	Future Plans
Existing System	Reports	Document	Problems
Priority	Benefits	Constraint	Management Information
Specify	Computer System	Confidential	Plan
Storage	Time	Operator	Volume
Feasibility	Requirement	Data Capture	Cost
Analyse	Schedule	Processes	ERD

Exercise 25   Databases

Relational	Foreign Key	DBMS	Primary Key
1NF	Table	UNF	Compound Key
2NF	Link	Attribute	3NF
Index	Integrity	Field	Independent
Search	Dependent	Entity	Key
Consistent	DML	Relational Database	SQL
Redundant	Relationship	Repetition	Secondary Key
File	Normalise	QBE	Normal
Unique	Database	Repeated Attribute	DDL

Exercise 26   Programming languages

Software	Interpreter	Imperative Language	Selection
High-Level Language	Assembler	Java	Third Generation
Compiler	Application Software	Declaration	Fortran
Machine Code	C++	Statements	Second Generation
Programming Language	Variables	Instructions	Visual Basic
C	Execution	Low Level Language	Iteration
System Software	First Generation	Assembly Language	Cobol
Pascal	Data Structures	Modules	Source Code
Translation	Ada	Modula-2	Object Code

Bug Hunts

These error-tracing exercises introduce collaborative work into programming, a topic that otherwise may involve much individual work. The exercises develop students' knowledge of programming language syntax and their debugging skills. These activities work best with small groups and are suitable for mixed-ability groups.

Each program handout contains ten or so deliberate errors. These range from simple typing errors, which the weaker students spot as readily as anyone, to fairly subtle logic errors that challenge the more able. Groups tend to compete to find the greatest number of errors in the program.

Each exercise features a particular programming technique that is usually indicated in the title. The order of the exercises roughly matches a teaching order for programming topics.

Delivery

1 Organise the class into groups of two or three and issue each student with a program listing.

2 Ask the students in each group to mark and correct all the errors they can find.

3 Tour the room encouraging participation and querying any misconceptions. A good way to stimulate the search is to announce the number of errors found so far by the leading groups. If a particular exercise is proving difficult, you can make it easier by telling the students which lines contain the errors.

4 When groups start to lose momentum, pair each one up with another group to share and discuss their findings.

5 In a final run through with the whole class, go through line by line asking for errors/corrections and confirming those that are right. There are likely to be false "errors" that need to be explained as carefully as the genuine ones.

As a variation, students can be asked to try out their amended code on a computer instead of being given the answers directly. A copy of the program for Exercise 28 is available on the publisher's website (www.payne-gallway.co.uk) for this purpose.

Timing

Typically this activity takes 15 to 20 minutes, but it can vary according to the expertise of the students. The first few exercises may take less time. More time is needed if you want students to try their amended programs on a computer.

Exercise 27   Variable Bug Hunt 1

The following Visual Basic program should take a price displayed in one text box, add VAT at 17½% and display the total in a second text box. It contains several errors. Circle as many errors as you can find. In each case, write a correct version alongside.

```
Explicit Option

Private cmdAddVat_Cluck()
Dim Price As Single
Din Vat As Single
Dim Total As Integer
Price = txtPrice,Text
Vat = (17.5 \ 100) * Price
Total = Price + Vet
txtDisplay.Text = Total
End Sub
```

Exercise 28   Variable Bug Hunt 2

The following Visual Basic program is intended to solve *any* equation of the form

$$ax + b = 0$$

Unfortunately, my little brother has been messing around with my computer and there are now several bugs in the program, which stop it working properly: find and correct them.

You can assume that the text boxes and the command button have been named correctly.

```
Option Implicit

Pirate Sub cmdSolve-Click()
Dim a As Integer
Dim b As Integer

a = txtA.Txt
b = txtB.Txt
x = x / a
x = -b
x = txtSolution.Text
Sink Sub
```

Exercise 29   Bug Hunt "For" Loop

The program below is written in Visual Basic version 5/6, which allows direct printing to a form. It should output a table for converting miles into kilometres, but contains a large number of errors.

Find the errors in the program. When you find an error, circle it and write a correct version alongside it.

```
Option Explicit
Private Sub Form_Loan()
    Dim Miles As Interger
    Dim Kilometres As Single
    Dim StartMiles As Integer; EndMiles As Integer
    Dim MilesIncrement As Integer
    Show Form1
    StartMiles = 10
    EndMales = 50
    MilesIncrement = 2
    Print "MILES", "KILOMETRES"
    For Miles From StartMiles To EndMiles By MilesIncrement
        Miles * 1.6 = Kilometres
        Print Miles, Kilometers
    Loop
End Sub
```

Score: 7 errors good   10 errors excellent!

Exercise 30   Squares and Cubes Bug Hunt

Find the bugs in the following Visual Basic program. Indicate each error and write corrections alongside.

```
Option Explicit
'program to print squares or cubes of numbers according to
'whether they are divisible by three. 10 numbers to be processed.

Private Sub Form_Load()
Dim Value As Integer
Dim ThreeCount As Intiger
Dim Start As Integer

Form1.Show
ThreeCount = 1
Form1.Print "number", "power"
Start = InputBox(Please enter a starting value")
Start = Value
Do
    Value = Value + 1
    If Value Mid 3 = 0 Then
        Form1.Print Value, Value * Value
        ThreeCount = ThreeCount + 1
    Else
        Form1.Print.Value, Value + Value + Value
    End If
Loop Until Value = 10 + Start
Form1,Print "There were " & ThreeCounties & " multiples of three."
And Sub
```

Score: 6 errors fair   8 good   10 excellent

Exercise 31   Guessing Game Bug Hunt

Find all the errors in the following Visual Basic program. Circle each error and write a correct version alongside.

```
Option Implicit
Dim Value Is Integer
Dim Goes Is Integer


Private Sub cmdGuess_Cluck()
Dum Guess Is Integer
Guess = txtGuess.Text
Goes + 1 = Goes
If Guess > Value Then
   lblDisplay.Caption = "Too High"
Else
   If Guess > Value Then
     lblDisplay.Caption = "Too Low"
   Else
     lblDisplay.Caption = "   YOU GOT IT !!!   " & It took " & Gos & " goes"
End If
txtGuess.Text = ""
txtGuess.SetFocus
End Sub




Private Sub Form-Load()
Randomize
Valve = Int(Rnd() * 100 + 1
Goes = 0
End Sub
```

Score: 7 errors fair   9 good   12 excellent

Exercise 32 Procedure Bug Hunt

The Visual Basic procedure *AddParity* should accept a string that consists of a space followed by seven binary digits, and it should replace the space with a parity bit. This modified string is returned to the calling procedure.

The procedure takes two parameters. The first parameter is the string; the second parameter indicates whether odd or even parity should be used.

Part of the calling routine is shown below, followed by procedure *AddParity*. Circle all the errors you can find and write correct versions alongside.

```
Private Sub cmdAddParity_Click()
Dim AByte As String * 8
Dim Even As Boolean
:
Call AddParity(Even, AByte)
:
End Sub


Public Sob AddParity(ByVal AWord As String, EvenParity Is Boolean)
Dim PBit As Integer
Dim Position As Integer
Dim EvenParity As Boolean

If EvenParity Then
    PBit = 0
Else
    PBit = 1
End It
For Position = 2 To 7
    If Mid(AWord, Position, 1) = "1" Then
        PBit = 1 - PBit
    End If
Next PBit
AByte = Format(PBit) & Right(AWord, 7)
End Sub
```

Score: 5 Fair   7 Good   9 Excellent

Exercise 33   Function Bug Hunt

The following is part of a Visual Basic program for managing darts scores. The procedure *cmdEnter_Click* is correct but the function after it contains a dozen errors. Find and mark each error or omission and write a correct version alongside.

```
Option Explicit

Private Sub cmdEnter_Click()
Dim Forename As String, Surname As String, Score As String

Forename = Trim(txtForeName.Text)
Surname = Trim(txtSurname.Text)
Score = Trim(txtScore.Text)
If ValidEntry(Forename, Surname, Score) Then
    lstLeague.AddItem Surname & " " & Forename & " " & Score
End If
End Sub


Public Function Valid Entry(Name1, Name2, AvScore As String) = Boolean
OK = True
If (Name1 <> "") Or (Name2 <> "") Then
    If IsNumeric(AvScare) Then
        If (AvScore <= 0) And (AvScore <= 180) Then
            OK = True
        Else
            MsgBox (Scores must be in the range 0 to 180 inclusive)
            txtScore = ""
            txtScore.SetFocus
        End
    Else
        MsgBox ("Please enter a valid number as the score")
        txtScore = ""
        txtScore.SetFocus
    End If
Else
    MsgBox ("Please enter both names")
End If
OK = ValidEntry
End Function
```

Score: 5 Fair   7 Good   10 Excellent

Exercise 34   Array Bug Hunt

The following is part of a Visual Basic program to select players for a football team and store them in an array. Find and mark as many bugs in the program as you can. Write corrections alongside.

```
Option Explicit

Dim Player(1 UpTo 11) As String
Dim TotalPicked As Integer


Private Sub cmdAdd_Click()        'Add a player to the team if not already picked
Dim NewPlayer As String
Dim Position As String
Dim Found As Boolean
NewPlayer = txtPlayer.Text
Found = False
Position = 1 To TotalPicked
    If NewPlayer = Player(TotalPicked) Then
        Fond = True
        MsgBox "This player has already been picked"
    End If
Next Position
If Found Then
    Player(TotalPicked) equals NewPlayer
    TotalPicked = TotalPicked + 1
End Sub


Private Sub Form_Load()      'Set up first two player names
Player[1] = "Banks"
Player(2) = Pele
TotalPickled = 2
End Sub
```

Score: 7 Fair   9 Good   12 Brilliant!

Exercise 35   Record Bug Hunt

The following code is part of a Visual Basic program that handles employee records. It contains a number of errors, but you may assume that form control names are correct. Mark as many errors as you can find and write correct versions alongside.

```
Option Explisit

Type EmployeeRecordType
    EmployeeNo As Integer
    Name As String * 15
    Job As Sting * 12
    DateEmployed As Date
End Type


Private Sub cmdEnter_Click()
Dim AnEmployee As EmployeeRecord
With An Employee
    .EmployeeNo = txtEmpNo.Text
    Name = txtName.Text
    Job = txtJob.Text
    DateEnployed = Date
EndWith
lstEmployees.AddItem .EmployeeNo & "   " .Name & .Job & .DateEmployed
End Sub
```

Score: 6 Fair   8 Good   10 Excellent

Exercise 36   File Handling Bug Hunt 1

The Visual Basic procedure *cmdDisplayFile_Click* should display the contents of a file of student data in a listbox; it is shown below, together with the relevant record declaration. You may assume that the record declaration is correct, but the procedure contains a number of errors.

Circle all the errors that you can find and write correct versions alongside.

```
Private Type StudentType
     IDNo As String * 6
     Name As String * 20
     TG As String * 5
     DoB As Date
End Type



Private Sub cmdDisplayFile_Click()
'read all records from disk, displaying them in list box
Din Student As StudentType
Dim NoOfRecords As Integer
Dim Count As Integer
Open "StuData.dat" For Random As #1
NoOfRecords = Len(1) / Len(Student)
For Count = 0 To NoOfRecord
     Read #1, , Student
     With Student
          lstStudents.AddItem .IDNo & " " & .Name & " " & TG & " " & .Age
Next
Shut #1
End Sub
```

Exercise 37 File Handling Bug Hunt 2

The Visual Basic procedure *cmdDelete_Click* should delete a student record
from a file. The record to be deleted has previously been selected from a list
box. The record definition is given below, followed by the procedure itself.
All deliberate errors are in the procedure. Circle as many errors as you can
find and write correct versions alongside.

```
Private Type StudentType
    IDNo As String * 6
    Name As String * 20
    TG As String * 5
    DoB As Date
End Type


Private Rub cmdDelete_Click()
Dim Student As StudentType
Dim NoOfRecords As Integer
Dim Count As Integer
Dim ToBeDeleted As String * 5
ToBeDeleted = Left(lstStudents.Text, 6)
Open "StuData.dat" For Random As #1 Len = Len(Student)
Open "NewStu.dat" For Random As #2 Len = Len(Student)
NoOfRecords = LOF(2) / Len(Student)
For Count = 1 To NoOfRecords
    Get #1, , Student
    If Student.IDNo = ToBeDeleted Then
        Write #1, , Student
Next Count
Close #1
Close #2
Delete "StuData.dat"
Rename "NewStu.dat" As "StuData.dat"
End Sub
```

Score: 5 fair   7 good   9 excellent

Exercise 38   File Handling Bug Hunt 3

Below is part of a Visual Basic file-handling program. It contains at least 16 errors. How many can you find?

```
Explicit Option

Private Typ StudentType
    IdNo As String * 8
    Name As String * 20
    TG As Strong * 5
    Age As Integer
End Type



Private Sub cmdFind_Click()
Dim Wanted As String * 6
Dam Student As StudentType
txtIDNo.Text = ""
txtName.Text = "
txtTG.Text = ""
txtAge.Text = ""
If txtFind.Text = "" Then
    MsgSox ("Please enter an ID Number")
Else
    Student = txtFind.Text
    Open "StuData.dat" For Random As #1 Len = Len(Wanted)
    While Not EOF(1)
        Get #2,  Student
        If Student.IdNo = Wanted Then
            txtIDNo.Text = Student.IdNo
            txtName.Text = Student.Name
            txtTG.Text = Student.TutorGroup
            Student.Age = txtAge.Text
    Loop
    Close #1
End Of
End Sub
```

Score: 10 Good   12 Excellent   16 Brilliant!

Exercise 39 Recursion Bug Hunt 1

The Fibonacci sequence of numbers (1, 1, 2, 3, 5, 8, 13 etc.) lies behind many naturally occurring patterns, particularly spiral patterns. Each term in the sequence (after the first two) is the sum of the two previous terms. In mathematical language:

$$term(n) = term(n-1) + term(n-2).$$

The following Visual Basic program uses a recursive function *Fib* in an attempt to generate terms of the sequence and display them in a listbox. It contains a number of errors. Find as many errors as you can, mark them on this sheet and write correct versions alongside.

Assume that the names given for the listbox, and for the text box used to input the number of terms, are correct.

```
Option Explicit


Private Sub cmdEnter_Click()
Dim Length As Long
Dim Index As Long
lstFibonacci.Cleer
Length = txtLength.Text
For Index = 1 To Length
    lstFibonacci.Add Fib(Length)
Next Index
End Sub


Public Function Fib(Term As Long)   Long
If Term < 2 Then
    Fib = 1
Else
    Fib = Fib(Term + 1) + Fib(Term + 2)
End Fun
```

Score: 4 Fair   6 Good   8 Excellent

Exercise 40   Recursion Bug Hunt 2

Find all the errors in the following Visual Basic program. The program should convert denary (decimal) numbers to binary. The form is shown below after the number 83 has been processed.

Assume that control names are correct.

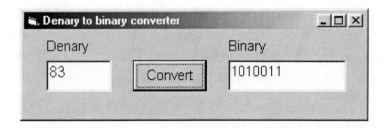

```
Option Explicit

Pullic Sub Readout(ByValue i As Integer)
txtBinary.Text = txtBinary.Text & (i Mod 2)
If i > 0
    Readout (i / 2)
End If
End Sub


Private Sub cmdConvert_Click()
Readabout (txtDenary.Text)
txtBinary.Text = ""
End Sub
```

Score: 4 fair   6 good   8 excellent

Exercise 41   Variable Bug Hunt

Find as many errors as you can in the following Pascal program. Circle each error and write a correct version alongside.

```
Program reading (Input, Output);
(Demonstrates variables and use of readln and writeln)

Var num1, num2 : Integer
        average, total : Real;

Began
Writeln ('What mark did you get for the first test?);
Writeln ('Enter the number and press <Enter>.');
Writeln;
Readln num1;
Writeln;
Writeln ('What was the mark for the second test?');
Writeln ('Enter this number and press <Enter> again.');
Writeln;
Readln (number2);
Writeln;
total := num1 + num2;
average = total / 2;
Writeln ('Your total mark is ' total :6:0);
Writeln ('Your average mark is ', mean :5:1);
End  {of reading}
```

Score: 6 fair   8 good   10 excellent

Exercise 42   Selection Bug Hunt

Find as many errors as you can in the following Pascal program. Circle each error and write a correct version alongside. The purpose of the program is to accept menu choices and then to output a statement such as "You have chosen rhubarb and custard" on a single line.

```
Program menu (Input, Output);
{Enters and confirms menu choice}
Var choice1, choice2 = Char;


Begin
Write ('Do you want rhubarb or pie? (R/P) ');
Readln (choice1);
Write('Do you want custard or ice cream? (C/I) ');
Readln (choice2);
If Not (choice1 In ['R', 'P']) Or (choice2 In ['C', 'I']) Then
    Writeln ('Your choice is not available.')
Else
    Begin
    Writ ('You have chosen ');
    If choice1 := R Then
        Write('rhubarb ');
    Else
        Write 'pie '
    If choice2 = 'C' Then;
        Writeln ('and custard.')
    Else;
        Writeln ('and ice cream.')
    End
End. {of menu}
```

Score: 6 fair   8 good   10 excellent

Exercise 43 Loopy Bug Hunt

Find as many errors as you can in the following Pascal program. Circle each error and write a correct version alongside.

```
Program MultiTable (Input Output);
{creates multiplication table}

Var Line, Column : Integer;

Begin
Write(How many rows? );
Readin (Limit);
Writeln;
Writeln (Limit, ' times table');
Writeln;
For Line :=1 To Limit Do;
      Begin
      Far Column := 1 To Limit Do;
            Write (Line * Column ;4);
      Writeln
Writeln;
Writeln ('Table completed. Press <Enter>');
Readln
End
```

Score: 6 fair   8 good   10 excellent

Exercise 44   Procedures Bug Hunt

The following is part of a Pascal program to analyse sentences. Find as many errors as you can in the procedure, circle them and write correct versions alongside. (Assume the main program is correct.)

```
Procedure count_chars (line : sentence)
{counts characters in a sentence, but not spaces}


Var    position; ch_count : Integer;


Begin
ch-count := 1;
For position := 1 To length(a_line)
    If line[position] <> ' ' Then;
        ch_count := ch_count + 1;
Wroteln('Excluding spaces, the sentence contains ', ch_count, ' characters');
End   {of procedure count_chars}


Begin   {main program analyse}
input_sentence (a_line);
count_chars (a_line);
End.   {of program analyse}
```

Score: 6 fair   8 good   9 excellent

Exercise 45   Array Bug Hunt

Find as many errors as you can in the following Pascal program. Circle each error and write a correct version alongside.

```
Program arrays (Input, Output);
{demonstrates arrays - very politely}

Var marklist : Array(1..5) As Integer;
    index = Integer;

For index := 1 To 5 Do
    Begin
    Write ('Enter a mark ') :
    Readln (marklist[n]);
    End
Writeln ('Thank you. You did do well!  Please press <Enter> to continue.');
Readln;
Writeln ('Your marks as entered:');
For index := 1 To 5 Do
    Write (marklist, ' ');
Writeln;
Writeln ('Please press <Enter> again');
Readln;
Writeln ('Thank you.  Now here they are in reverse order .......');
For index := 5 To 1 Do
    Write (marklist[index], ' ');
Writeln;
Writeln ('Please press <Enter> to finish');
Readin;
End. {of arrays}
```

Score: 6 fair   8 good   10 excellent

Exercise 46   File Bug Hunt

Find as many errors as you can in the following Pascal program. Circle each error and write a correct version alongside. (Assume that the horizontal spacing of the output is correct.)

```
Program listcars (Input, Output);
{list contents of file cardata.dat}


Tipe
     colours   = String[8];
     car_descr = String[10];
     car : Record
               make  : car_descr;
               doors : Integer;
               colour: colors;
          End.


Var carinfo      : file of cars;
      vehicle      : car;


Begin
Assign (carinfo, 'cardata.dat');                    {link to physical file}
Rest (carinfo);
Writeln ('                Make      No. of Doors      Colour');
Writeln;
While Eof(carinfo) Do
     Start
     Read (carinfo vehicle);
     Write (car.make:24);
     Write (vehicle.door:15);
     Writeln (vehicle.colour:15);
     End;
Writeln;
Writeln('Press <Enter> to continue');
Readln
End.  {of listcars}
```

Score: 7 fair   9 good   12 excellent

Spot the Difference

Whereas a clear understanding of language syntax is needed to complete Bug Hunts successfully, this is not true of Spot the Difference. These exercises can be used in at least two ways:

- to help beginners who are still very unsure of themselves

- to illustrate the similarities and differences between programming languages by getting students to engage with a language they have not met before.

Languages covered are Pascal, Visual Basic, C and Java. The last exercise (Ex. 52) is likely to prove harder than the others, and may be best reserved for the most able students.

Delivery (similar to Bug Hunts)

1 Organise the class into groups of two or three and issue each student with a program listing.

2 Ask each group to mark all the errors they can find.

3 Tour the room encouraging participation. As with bug hunts, announcing the number of errors found by the leading groups can stimulate further activity.

4 When groups start to lose momentum, pair each one up with another group to share and discuss their findings.

5 In a final run through with the whole class, go through line by line asking for errors.

Timing

Allow around 15 minutes.

Exercise 47 Visual Basic Spot the Difference

The Visual Basic in listing A is correct. Circle the 10 errors in listing B.

Listing A

```
Dim Score(1 To 10) As Integer
Dim N As Integer

Private Sub Command1_Click()
Text1.Text = Av(Score, N)
End Sub

Private Sub Form_Load()
Score(1) = 34
Score(2) = 36
Score(3) = 17
Score(4) = 50
Score(5) = 14
N = 5
End Sub

Public Function Av(ByRef Data, c As _
Integer) As Single
Dim i As Integer
Dim Total As Integer
For i = 1 To c
    Total = Total + Data(i)
Next
Av = Total / c
End Function
```

Listing B

```
Dim Score(1 To 10) Is Integer
Dim N As Integer

Private Sub Command1_Click()
Text1.Text = Av(Score)
End Sub

Private Sub Form_Lead()
Score(1) = 34
Score(2) = 36
Score(3) = 17
Score(4) = 50
Scorn(5) = 14
N = 5
And Sub

Public Function Av(ByRef Data, c As _
Integer) As Single
Dum Total As Integer
For i = 1 To c
    Total + Score(i) = Total
Av = Total / c
End Function
```

Exercise 48   Pascal Spot the Difference 1

This Pascal procedure analyses a positive number to see if it is prime:

```
PROCEDURE analyse(number : LONGINT);
VAR divisor, limit : LONGINT;
        prime : BOOLEAN;


BEGIN
prime := true;
limit := trunc(sqrt(number) +1);
divisor := 1;
REPEAT
    divisor := divisor + 1;
    IF number MOD divisor = 0 THEN
        prime := false;
UNTIL (NOT prime) OR (divisor >= limit);
WRITE (number, ' is ');
IF prime OR (number = 2) THEN
    WRITELN ('PRIME')
ELSE
    WRITELN ('not prime');
END {of analyse};
```

Find the errors in the following version. There are at least 13!

```
PROCEDURE analyse(number : LONGLNT);
VAR divisor : LONGINT;
        prime : BOOLEAN;


BEGIN
prime := true;
limit := trunc(sqrt(number) -1);
divisor := 1;
REPEAT;
    divisor = divisor + 1;
    IF number MOD divisor := 0 THEN
        prim := false;
UNTIL (NOT prime) OR (divisor <= limit);
WRITE (number, ' is ')
IF prime AND (number = 2) THEN;
    WRITELN (PRIME)
ELSE
END {of analyse};
```

THE COLLEGE OF WEST ANGLIA

Exercise 49   Pascal Spot the Difference 2

Here is an extract from a correct Pascal program:

```
Program journey (Input, Output);
Var letter : Char;

Begin
Write ('Enter a letter ');
Readln (letter);
While letter In ['N','E','W','S'] Do
      Begin
      Case letter Of
            'N' : Writeln('North');
            'E' : Writeln('East');
            'W' : Writeln('West');
            'S' : Writeln('South')
            End;
      Write ('Enter a letter ');
      Readln (letter)
      End
End.
```

Task 1   Decide what the above program does.

Task 2   Correct the eight deliberate errors in the following similar program:

```
Program flight (Input, Output)
Var direction : Char;

Begin
Write ('Enter a letter ');
Reedln (direction);
While direction In ['U','D','S'] Do;
      Begin
            Case direction Of
            'U' : Writeln(Up);
            'D' : Writeln('Down');
            'S' : Writeln('Steady')
            End
      Write (Enter a letter ');
      Readln (letter)
      End
End
```

Exercise 50   Java Spot the Difference

Here is an extract from a correct Java Program:

```
System.out.print ("Enter a positive integer : ");
int value = Input.readInt();
while (value <= 0)
{
     System.out.println ("You must enter a positive value");
     System.out.print ("Enter a positive integer : ");
     value = Input.readInt();
}
System.out.println ("The square of your number is " + (value * value) );
```

Task 1   Decide what this section of program does.

Task 2   Correct the errors in the following similar program:

```
System.out.print ("Enter a negative integer : );
int value = Input.readInt();
while (value >= 0);
}
     System.out.println ("You must enter a negative value")
     value = Input.println();
     System.out.print ("Enter a negative integer : ")
{
System.out.println ("The square of your number is " & value * value) );
```

Exercise 51   C Spot the Difference 1

Here is an extract from a correct C Program

```
do {
    printf("\nEnter two numbers: ");
    scanf("%f %f",&x,&y);
    if (y == 0.0)
        printf("You cannot divide by zero\n");
    else  {
        quotient = x / y;
        printf("The quotient is %f \n",quotient);
    }
    printf("Press any key to continue or 'f' to finish\n");
} while (getch() != 'f');
```

Task 1   Decide what the above section of program does.

Task 2   Find and correct the eight deliberate errors in the following similar program:

```
do {
    printf("\nEnter two numbers: ")
    scant("%f %f",&x,&y);
    if (y < x) then
        difference = y - x;
    else;  {
        difference = x - y;
        printf("The absolute difference is \n",difference);
    }
    printf("Press any key to continue or 'e' to end\n");
} while (getch() != 'f');
```

Exercise 52   C Spot the Difference 2

Task 1   Study the following section of a C program and decide what it does:

```
{
    int  a,c,j;

    printf("Table generator\n");
    printf("\n");
    printf("Enter a whole number between 1 and 10 ");
    scanf("%d", &a);
    for(c = 1; c <= a; c++)
        {
        for (j = 1; j <=a; j++)
            printf("%4d", c*j);
        printf("\n"); }
    do
        printf("Press 'f' to finish\n");
    while (getch() != 'f');
}
```

Task 2   Find and correct the eight deliberate errors in the following similar program:

```
{
    int  a,c,j;

    printf("Difference Table generator\n");
    printf("\n")
    printf("Enter a whole number between 1 and 10 ");
    scare("%d", &a);
    printf("     ");
    for(c = 1; c <= a; c++)
        printf("%4d", c);
        printf("/n");
    for(c := 1; c <= a; c++)
        {
        printf("%4d" c);
        for (j = 1; j <=a; j - -)
            printf("%4d", c-j);
        printf("\n");
    do
        printf("Press 'f' to finish\n");
    while (gotcha() != 'f');

}
```

Crosswords and Cross-numbers

These exercises are useful as a way of varying activities during revision and making it more fun. The exercises can be done individually, but if students work in pairs they learn from each other and find it more enjoyable. The element of crosschecking that is built into the format of a crossword also introduces a degree of self-assessment.

The cross-numbers provide a convenient means of giving students extra practice with binary numbers. Many students who dislike conventional exercises enjoy these.

Delivery

1 Divide the class into pairs and give each student a copy of the worksheet.

2 When the first pairs finish, check their answers or give them a copy of the answers to check for themselves.

3 When all, or nearly all, have finished, run through the answers with the whole class.

Timing

Allow up to 15 minutes for the crosswords, depending on student ability. Allow at least half an hour for the binary cross-numbers, which have more questions to solve.

Exercise 53 Introduction to Computing

Across

3 a character code (5)

6 a character code (7)

7 a binary digit (3)

8 a type of data used a lot on spreadsheets (6)

12 a common input device (5)

13 the number system used by computers (6)

14 an 'A' Level subject related to Computing (2)

Down

1 the commonest output device? (3)

2 a common output device (7)

4 these are usually represented by a very large number of bits (6)

5 to work with this kind of data you could use headphones (5)

7 eight bits (4)

9 where a running program is held (6)

10 this type of data is stored using a character code (4)

11 the number base used by humans (3)

Exercise 54 'AS' Computing Revision

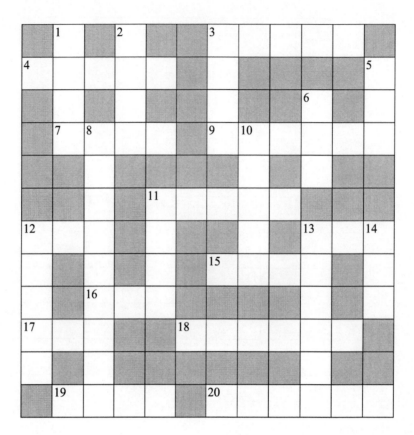

Across

3   data structure used to reverse lists (5)

4   device that converts between digital and analogue (5)

7   a type of bus (4)

9   a bit added for checking (6)

11   a type of operating system (5)

12   a means of interrogating a database (abbr) (3)

13   a volatile component of main memory (3)

15   a collection of records (4)

16   a number representation (abbr) (3)

17   the location of data on the Internet (abbr) (3)

18   a type of graphics (6)

19   a data structure (4)

20   system of character encoding (6)

Down

1   the basic unit of data handled by a processor (4)

2   type of data stored using a character code (4)

3   a bit added to end of data transmitted asynchronously (4)

5   a field used for indexing (3)

6   eight of these make a byte (3)

8   program that translates low-level code into machine code (9)

10   a character code (5)

11   ---- rate; the number of signal changes per second (4)

12   data structure much used by printers (5)

13   a data structure that can combine data of different types (6)

14   an operation giving the remainder after division (3)

Exercise 55 Programming Languages

Across

3   a simple language based on 4 down (5)

5   a logic programming language (6)

6   an OOP language (9)

8   a language often used for concurrent processes (3)

9   a structured language (6)

12   often considered the first highly structured language (5)

13   a scripting language (4)

Down

1   a general language often associated with the Web (4)

2   a language used for artificial intelligence (4)

4   the first widely used high-level scientific programming language (7)

7   a language used for real-time systems (7)

10   the first widely used commercial high-level language (5)

11   a language best known for its use of turtle graphics (4)

Exercise 56   Database and Systems Development

Across

1   the language used to define a database (abbreviation) (3)

4   software that controls access to a database (abbreviation) (4)

7   the "C" of BCNF (4)

9   ------code used to define algorithms (6)

10   the "E" of EAR (6)

11   testing by selected potential users (4)

13   SQL term used to define order of output (7)

14   the smallest possible unit of data (3)

15   the "DB" of DBMS (8)

16   another name for *user interface* (3)

17   often the first word in an SQL statement (6)

20   testing, where modules are combined (11)

Down

2   a diagram that can be used to document an existing or proposed system (3)

3   system conversion done in stages (6)

5   feasibility ----- (5)

6   a first version of a system (9)

8   the quickest changeover method (6)

12   the "A" of EAR (9)

14   the "B" of BCNF (5)

15   comes after Analysis in the systems development cycle (6)

18   the simplest user interface style (abbreviation) (3)

19   a logic operator often used in queries (3)

Exercise 57   Processor and Low Level Programming

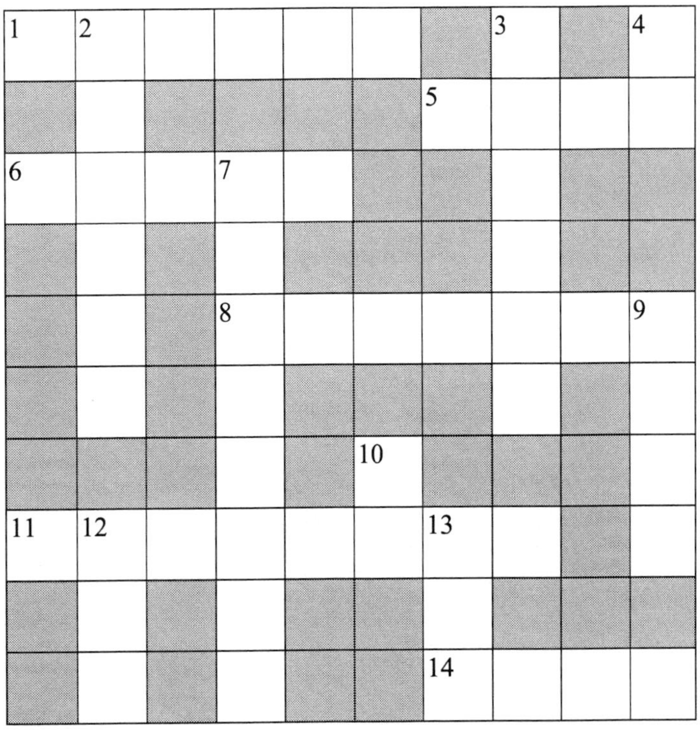

(crossword grid)

Across

1   this type of instruction may be conditional (6)

5   a type of processor with a large instruction set (4)

6   an instruction that accesses main memory (5)

8   a type of shift (7)

11 an addressing mode that makes a wide address space available (8)

14 a type of processor with a streamlined instruction set (4)

Down

2   a type of shift that preserves all bits in a register (6)

3   the "normal" addressing mode (6)

4   the register that stores the address of the next instruction (2)

7   relocatable code uses this addressing mode for branching (8)

9   an instruction that accesses main memory (4)

10 all instructions must go through this cycle (2)

12 a logical operator (3)

13 this register holds the instruction being processed (3)

Exercise 58 Binary Number Puzzle 1

1		2		░	░	3	4		
	░		░	5		░		░	░
6		7			8			░	9
	░			░	10		11		
	░	12	13			14			
	░		15		16				
17			18		░				
░	19			░	20		21		
░			22		░				
23			░	░	24				

Across

1　2 to the power of 10

3　13 in binary

5　111000 in decimal

6　18 in binary

8　1000110 in decimal

10　1111 in decimal

11　Maximum number of items in a 5-level binary tree

12　Maximum number of items in a 10-level binary tree

15　Eleven in binary

17　12 down – 20 down (answer in binary)

18　1010110 in decimal

19　1000000 in decimal

20　29 in binary

22　1100001 in decimal

23　bytes in a kilobyte

24　9 in binary

Down

1　162 in binary

2　11100110 in decimal

4　18 across – 8 across – 10
　(answer in binary)

5　110010 in decimal

7　8 across – 19 across (in binary)

8　1001011 in decimal

9　100000000 minus 1 (in binary)

10　10000010 in decimal

12　10011 in decimal

13　11011000 in decimal

14　1011011 in decimal

16　5 across – 5 down + 1 (in binary)

18　1010100 in decimal

19　1001100100 in decimal

20　1010 + 111 (answer in decimal)

21　10110100 in decimal

Exercise 59   A2 Computing   Binary Number Puzzle

1		2				3	4		
			5						
6		7			8			9	
				10		11			
	12	13			14				
		15	16						
17		18							
	19		20		21				
		22							
23				24					

Assume 8 bit binary numbers are in 2s complement form unless told otherwise.

Across

1   $1\frac{3}{4}$ in binary
3   D hexadecimal converted to binary
5   00101100 in decimal
6   22 in binary
8   01001000 in decimal
10   00010010 in decimal
11   01110001 $_{BCD}$ in decimal
12   -6 in 4 bit binary
15   the exponent (in binary) when 0.25 is stored in floating point form
17   the exponent (in binary) when 3.5 is stored in floating point form
18   00001011 in decimal
19   11110111 in decimal
20   -3 in 5 bit binary
22   01010000 $_{BCD}$ in decimal
23   10001111 in decimal
24   $2\frac{1}{2}$ in binary

Down

1   -94 in 8 bit binary
2   $1^1/_2$ in binary
4   7A (hexadecimal) in decimal
5   00101000 in decimal
7   the exponent (in binary) when 35 is stored in floating point form
8   4 down – 5 across in decimal
9   minus 1 in 8 bit binary
10   01100001 – 01011100 in binary
12   11100110 + 00011101 in binary
13   01101111 in decimal
14   00101001 in decimal
16   the exponent (in binary) when 17 is stored in floating point form
18   00010011 in binary
19   10111001 in decimal
20   00111110 +11000100
21   384 in hexadecimal

Exercise 60   Hexadecimal Number Puzzle

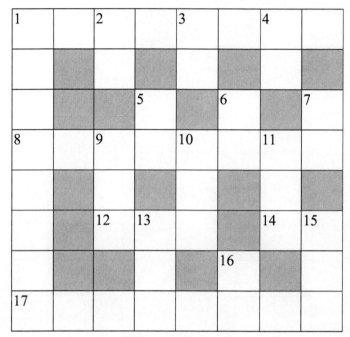

Convert hexadecimal numbers to binary and binary numbers to hexadecimal.

Across

1   BA

8   EB

12   101110101100

14   10101011

17   D2

Down

1   95

2   11010

3   00011111

4   011000

5   11100000

6   1010000

7   10010001

9   111011011

10   000100001100

11   111101010

13   101001110001

15   101100000000

16   10000000

Quick Quizzes

The *quick quiz* is another activity that can be used for a short topic review. It serves a similar purpose to a question and answer session, but has the advantage of fully involving every student. It provides a crisp start or clear conclusion to a lesson. Used at the start of a lesson, it is a good way of focussing attention on key points made in previous sessions. Used at the end of a lesson, it enables students to assess how much they have learnt.

The activity needs to be brisk, so answers should be short and there should not be too many questions. Eight questions are ample.

The purpose of the exercise is self-assessment, not formal assessment by the teacher. It pays to observe how any weaker students are coping during the quiz, but it can be counter-productive to collect marks. Once students recognise that they are not being judged, they are likely to regard the quiz as a positive opportunity, not a threat.

This book contains just a few examples for you to try out. It is easy to make up more quizzes of your own if you want to make them a regular feature of lessons. Consider starting with an easy question to get things going and ending with one that creates an opening for follow-up discussion of a related topic.

Delivery

1. Make sure that every student has something to write on (an A5 sized piece of scrap paper will do).

2. Read each question in turn, allowing time for students to write down the answer.

3. Run through the answers.

4. Praise those who have done well (say, 6 or more correct out of 8) and encourage the others to note down the things they need to revise later.

Timing

Ten minutes should be ample.

Exercise 61   Binary Quick Quiz

	Question	Answer
0	Write down the number five in binary	1 0 1
1	Write down fifteen in binary	1 1 1 1 (note: 16 - 1)
2	Write down thirty in binary	1 1 1 1 0 (note: double 15)
3	How many different patterns of 0s and 1s can be made using 4 binary digits?	16 (2^4)
4	How many different patterns of 0s and 1s can be made using 5 binary digits?	32 (2^5)
5	What is the largest integer that can be written in binary using 5 digits?	31
6	Originally ASCII codes used 7 bits. How many different characters could be stored?	128 (2^7)
7	A kilobyte is 1024 bytes not 1000. What does the number 1024 look like in binary?	1 followed by 10 zeroes ("Give yourself half a mark if you wrote '1 followed by a lot of zeroes' ")

Possible follow up discussion points:

- the need for a larger range of character codes
- why 1 Kb = 1024 bytes
- "Why were the questions numbered zero to seven?"

Exercise 62   Data Structures Quick Quiz

	Question	Answer
0	Name a First In First Out data structure.	A queue
1	What data structure is associated with the operations "Pop" and "Push"?	A stack
2	What data structure uses an index to identify individual elements?	An array
3	Name a data structure that uses pointers	A tree or a linked list
4	What data structure can be circular or linear?	A queue
5	How deep must a binary tree be to hold 25 items of data?	At least five levels deep
6	What data structure can be used to help sort a list of items into order?	A binary tree
7	Name a data structure that allows fast retrieval of data	Any of: array, hash table, binary tree

Possible follow up discussion point:

- Which data structure permits the fastest data retrieval?

Exercise 63   Networks Quick Quiz

	Question	Answer
0	What does IP stand for?	Internet Protocol
1	Name a type of network with no servers.	Peer-to-peer
2	Name a type of networking in which messages are split into sections that travel independently.	Packet-switching
3	Name a term that means *to transmit several streams of data on the same communication line.*	Multiplexing
4	Name a device that uses IP addresses to forward messages.	A router
5	What protocol is used to transmit web pages across the Internet?	HTTP
6	What is the SMTP protocol used for?	E-mail
7	Out of ring, bus and star, which is the most secure topology to use for a local area network?	Star

Possible follow up discussion point:

- network security.

Exercise 64   OOP Quick Quiz

	Question	Answer
0	What does OOP stand for?	Object Oriented Programming
1	What is the name for the principle of combining data with all of the operations that can be carried out on that data?	Encapsulation
2	What is the name for the principle that allows two different subclasses of the same class to implement the same method in different ways?	Polymorphism
3	What is the name for the principle by which members of a class automatically take on properties and methods of a parent class?	Inheritance
4	What is the name for a class that has the attributes and methods of a "parent" class?	Subclass
5	What term is used to mean *a particular object created from a class*?	An instance
6	What term means *an action associated with an object*?	A method
7	Name an object-oriented programming language.	C++, Java, Modula-2, Eiffel, Smalltalk, etc

Flying Form

A Team Project Using Procedures in Visual Basic

This exercise gives students an opportunity to work together on program development and to experience, in a very practical way, the benefits of a modular programming approach. Each student has to develop a different procedure in order to contribute to the final result – a form that bounces round the computer screen changing colour and size as it goes, rather like a screen saver. Each student's program can be run independently, but it is only when the work is combined that the full visual effect is obtained.

This particular application avoids the need for parameter passing, and so aids simplicity, but its main advantage is that it is very visual. Students find this project very enjoyable.

Although the program is in Visual Basic it should be readily adaptable to other visual programming languages. One version of the finished program can be downloaded from the publisher's website for demonstration.

Delivery

1. Before you start, you will need to ensure that students have a method of passing code that has been completed and tested from one student to another. On a networked system, email is likely to be easiest method, if it is available.

2. Organise the students into groups of three, dividing any "experts" among the groups. If the class size is not a multiple of three, it is possible for two students to share the three initial tasks between them.

3. Distribute the student instructions. These consist of two pages that can be printed back-to-back.

4. Each group needs to decide who will take on which task. The most difficult task is the one for changing colours, the easiest is adapting *MoveSideways* to move vertically. If students differ in ability, some guidance may be needed to ensure that they each get the most appropriate task. Insist that, before they start, they plan how the program will be put together, and by whom.

5. Get the students to study the original code carefully before they attempt to write their own procedures. Make sure they keep exactly to the instructions for creating the form.

6. It is important that students do not get too tied down, so be ready with hints if they are needed. Knowledge of how to use the Mod operator to cycle through a set of values (to feed into the RGB function) can help with *ChangeColour*.

7. As groups complete the three initial tasks, encourage them to demonstrate their work and then to try adding extra features of their own. Two suggested enhancements are given at the end of the student worksheet.

Timing

Allow at least an hour to make sure that every group succeeds with the initial tasks. The time can be reduced a little by entering the outline program in advance, but if this is done it is very important to make sure that students understand the code properly before they start to change it.

Exercise 65 Flying Form

The use of procedures to structure a program has many advantages. Onc of these is to make it easy for a team of programmers to work together on a large project. Each programmer can be given a separate task to carry out. If this task is written as a procedure it can be developed separately then pasted into the "master" program. Provided that the programmers each use local variables in their own procedures, they can work quite independently.

For this mini project you need to work in a team of three. You should each start a new Visual Basic project and set up a form containing a label and a timer.

The Width property of the form <u>must</u> be set to 3000 and the Height set to 2000.

The label must be called lblName, its Font property set to MS Sans Serif size 24 and its Alignment property set to "Center". Set its Caption to "Hello !" and make it nearly as wide as the form.

The Interval property of the Timer must be set to 10.

You then need to enter the following code:

```
Option Explicit

Public Sub MoveSideways()
    Dim count As Integer
    Dim change As Integer
    Static GoingRight As Boolean
    If (Form1.Left + Form1.Width) > 10000 Then
        GoingRight = False
    End If
    If Form1.Left <= 0 Then
        GoingRight = True
    End If
    If GoingRight Then
        change = 1
    Else
        change = -1
    End If
    For count = 1 To 100
        Form1.Left = Form1.Left + change
        DoEvents
    Next count
End Sub
```

```
Private Sub Form_Load()
    Form1.Show
End Sub

Private Sub Timer1_Timer()
    Call MoveSideways
    Call MoveVertically
    Call ChangeColour
    Call ChangeSize
End Sub

Public Sub MoveVertically()
End Sub

Public Sub ChangeColour()
End Sub

Public Sub ChangeSize()
End Sub
```

The principle of the program is very simple. Whenever the timer is called, it calls up each of the subprocedures *MoveSideways, MoveVertically, ChangeColour* and *ChangeSize.* As it stands, only the first procedure does anything: it moves the form from side to side. This first procedure has been written for you so that it can be used as a pattern for the others. Each member of the team should write <u>one</u> of the missing procedures.

The completed form should drift around the screen, bouncing off the sides and changing colour and size as it goes.

What to do

1   Agree which procedure each person will write and whose copy is the "master" version.

2   Enter the basic program into your own machine and test it to see how it works.

3   Add your procedure to your copy of the program. Test it. When you are sure that it works, copy your procedure to the "master" version.

To put the complete program together you need a way of exchanging code such as email or copying and pasting your new procedure into a Notepad or WordPad file, saving it on a floppy disk and giving it to the person with the master copy.

The aim is to get a complete working version of the program, without anyone having to write more than one new procedure.

Notes on procedure *MoveSideways*

The first **If** statement reverses the direction of travel when the right hand edge of the form reaches position 10000. You may want to vary this number depending on the resolution of your screen.

The second **If** statement reverses the direction when the form reaches the left hand edge of the screen.

DoEvents forces the computer to update the screen before continuing. This makes motion a little smoother.

Note that the variable **GoingRight** is declared as **Static**; this is so that each time the procedure is called it remembers which way it was going last time. If it was set up using a Dim statement, the value would be reset every time the procedure was called.

Hints for procedure *MoveVertically*

This procedure should move the form up or down the screen. It should mirror **MoveSideways** very closely. Use a variable **GoingDown** instead of **GoingRight**. Use the form properties **Top** and **Height** instead of **Left** and **Width**.

Hints for procedure *ChangeColour*

This procedure should change the colour of the form. It can be shorter than the first two. Only change the colour by a small amount each time the procedure is called; the **RGB** function allows you to do this. You might like to change the text colour of the label as well as the background colour of the form.

Hints for procedure *ChangeSize*

This procedure should change both the width and height of the form, but preferably keep it the same shape. It can be based on the same principles as **MoveSideways**, but you need to test for the value of **Form.Width** instead of **Form.Left**. Suggested limits for the width are 2000 and 4000. You will need to think carefully about how to keep the shape the same.

Other tasks

If there is time, try adding more procedures of your own. One might change the caption of the label to the name of each team member in turn. Another might make the form disappear when it enters a certain area on the screen but reappear when it moves out of that area.

Logic Programming

This exercise gives students extra practice at working in a logic programming language. It is assumed that they are familiar with logic programming and have had some experience of working with and interpreting programs written in Prolog or a Prolog-like language.

Delivery

1.   Divide the class into groups of three or four students. The groups do not have to be the same size, but *there must be an even number of groups.*

2.   Give each student a worksheet. Half of the groups should receive Worksheet A, and the other half should receive Worksheet B. Make sure that each group is happy with its scenario. If necessary, you can change the topic to suit the interests of the group. "Football" can be replaced by any team sport, or, at a pinch, any team activity. "Cars" can be replaced by some other commodity, such as mobile phones or games consoles.

3.   Make clear what each team has to do, then allow the groups 20 minutes to devise their facts and rules. The sample statements on the worksheets are only examples, and are not intended to be incorporated into the students' own programs.

4.   Tour the room to deal with any uncertainties or misunderstandings and encourage everyone to join in. It may be necessary to push along any groups that are being slow, to ensure that they all finish at about the same time. If members of a group race ahead, encourage them to try making their system more challenging, but resist any pleas to be allowed more than 20 statements. (Note that 20 is the limit for facts and rules combined, not for each type of statement.)

5.   As groups complete Task 2, pair them off with another group (a Group A with a Group B in each case) to do Tasks 3 and 4. Tell them to study the other team's statements carefully before attempting to answer the queries. Emphasise that they cannot challenge any of the facts and rules. If a statement says that Ronaldo plays for England, then for the purpose of this exercise he does play for England!

6.   When the groups have finished, have a brief "plenary" session to see what the students feel they have learnt.

Timing

Allow an hour for the whole activity.

Exercise 66   Logic Programming (A)

1.   Devise a set of 15 to 20 statements that give facts and rules relating to footballers.

Possible facts:

- Henry can shoot.

- Henry plays for Luton Town.

Possible rule:

- If a player can shoot and plays for Luton Town then he scores many goals.

Set out these statements in standard Prolog format. For example, you might write the fact "Campbell can tackle" as

```
has_skill(Campbell, can_tackle)
```

and the rule "If Y can tackle and Y is reliable then Y can defend" as

```
has_role(Y, can_defend) IF has_skill(Y,can_tackle) AND
has_skill(Y, reliability).
```

At least one rule should contain an **AND**.

2.   Devise 5 queries for your system, in standard Prolog format, to test another group of students.

For example

```
? has_role(X, can_defend)
```

should generate a list of potential defenders.

3.   Exchange work with a group that has done another topic and attempt to answer their queries.

4.   Mark the other group's answers. Discuss any ambiguities or misunderstandings that have shown up. Could any of your facts or rules have been better expressed?

Exercise 66   Logic Programming (B)

1.   Devise a set of 15 to 20 statements that give facts and rules relating to cars.

Possible facts:

   A Vectra is made by Vauxhall.

   A Vauxhall car is made in Britain.

Possible rule:

   If a car is British then it is cheap to insure.

Set out these statements in standard Prolog format. For example, you might write the fact "A Vauxhall car is made in Britain" as

```
is_made_in(Vauxhall, Britain)
```

and the rule "If a car type is made in country Y and cars made in Y are reliable then the car will hold its value" as

```
holds_value (X) IF is_made_in (X, Y) AND is_reliable_country(Y)
```

At least one rule should contain an **AND**.

2.   Devise five queries for your system, in standard Prolog format, to test another group of students.

For example

```
? made_by(X, Vauxhall)
```

should generate a list of cars made by Vauxhall.

3.   Exchange work with a group that has done another topic and attempt to answer their queries.

4.   Mark the other group's answers. Discuss any ambiguities or misunderstandings that have shown up. Could any of your facts or rules have been better expressed?

Applications of Computing

Most examination boards require students to have an understanding of the broad range of computer applications and may set questions based on some application that is described to the candidate.

This is an area with obvious scope for investigation by students, but they do need a framework to help structure their investigation. The attached worksheet uses six headings based on the AQA specification.

Students also need sources of information. A first-hand investigation is ideal, but is likely to be time-consuming and difficult to arrange. Other sources include videos, such as the series produced by TV Choice Ltd, and the wealth of information on the Internet. At the time of writing, the following sites give helpful information for the systems listed on the worksheet:

congestion charging:	http://www.tfl.gov.uk/tfl/cclondon/cc_fact_sheet_enforcement.shtml
games consoles:	http://entertainment.howstuffworks.com/video-game3.htm
GPS systems:	http://www.trimble.com/gps/index.html
banking:	http://money.howstuffworks.com/atm.htm
	http://www.apacs.org.uk/about_apacs/htm_files/chequecred.htm
booking systems:	http://www.hrcsystem.com/uk/
	http://www.reynard.co.uk/trags.pdf
flight control:	http://www.hamiltonsundstrandcorp.com/hsc/details/0,3797,CLI1_DIV22_ETI3019,00.html

Other subjects for investigation can be substituted according to the resources available.

Delivery

1   Decide whether you want students to work individually or in groups.

2   Issue worksheets and run through the analysis headings to make sure that everyone understands what you want them to do. Running through an example topic can help.

3   Set a deadline for reports to be completed.

As a possible variation, particularly where students are working in groups, ask them to prepare an on-screen presentation. The best presentations can be added to the school or college intranet for the benefit of other students.

Timing

Allow at least two hours of lesson and homework time for this activity, more if you want students to prepare presentations.

Exercise 67　Applications of Computing

As an 'A' Level student, you are expected to develop an appreciation of how computers are used in areas such as science, industry, commerce, leisure, design, communication, embedded systems and artificial intelligence. The application of Computing to a particular context can be analysed under the following headings, based on the AQA specification:

1　Purpose

Exactly what is the purpose of the application? How does it fit into the overall goals of the organisation? How important is it to the achievement of those goals?

2　Information

What information is processed by the system? What are the inputs, outputs, storage requirements and major processes involved?

3　User Interface

What are the specific user interface needs and how are they met? How does the system measure up to the principles of good interface design?

4　Communication Requirements

What communication needs are there? How are they achieved?

5　Satisfaction of Needs

To what extent does the application satisfy:

　　(a) the needs of the organisation?　　　　(b) the needs of individuals?

6　Wider consequences

What are the economic, social, legal and ethical consequences of the application and the way that it has been implemented? What are the effects of software failure, errors in transactions and poor system specification?

Choose one of the following systems to investigate. Write a summary of your findings under the six headings Purpose, Information, User Interface, Communication Requirements, Satisfaction of Needs and Wider Consequences.

A　A traffic congestion charging system, such as the one introduced in London.

B　A games console.

C　Geographical positioning systems.

D　The systems that handle customer accounts for a major high street bank.

E　A hotel booking system.

F　The flight control system on an aircraft.

Binary Number Investigation

Exercise 68 uses the program *Binary Counter* to introduce the two's complement representation of negative numbers. This program can be downloaded from the publisher's website www.payne-gallway.co.uk, and runs under the Windows operating system.

As well as the program, the worksheet and access to computers, students will require paper to write down rough working and to record their answers.

See the answer page for Exercise 68 for details of what students are expected to discover.

Delivery

Decide whether you want students to work individually or in pairs; the latter is recommended because it encourages them to discuss their findings.

Get students to load the program. Issue worksheets and tour the room while they work through the tasks. Check carefully that they have completed the table correctly before going on to the later tasks, and make sure that they write all eight bits down for *every* number.

The last two or three tasks may go better if pairs of students combine to form bigger groups. One spokesperson from each group can then report their findings to the whole class.

When the groups have finished, hold a whole-class review of the findings. Identify and reinforce key points carefully.

Timing

Allow around 30 minutes for the whole activity.

Exercise 68   Investigating Binary Numbers

The program *Binary Counter* counts using binary numbers. The controls allow it to count either forwards or backwards. It can be run automatically, or run manually in single steps. Starting values can be set by clicking on individual digits.

1   Load and run *Binary Counter*. Run it in automatic mode and note what happens when it reaches its maximum value. Stop the program, put it into reverse with a starting value of 00001111 and run it in automatic mode again. Make a note of what happens when it passes zero.

2   How many different numbers can be stored in an 8 bit store?

    If only positive numbers are stored, what is the range of numbers available?

We can either regard all the available bit patterns as positive numbers or use some for positive and some for negative values. If we do the latter and our counter is to work smoothly, we want the number before zero to represent -1, the number before that to be -2, and so on. **This is the system known as *two's complement* notation.**

3   Set the counter to manual mode and use it to help you complete the table below to show the two's complement representation of numbers between -7 and 7.

denary	8 bit binary	denary	8 bit binary
0	00000000	0	00000000
1		-1	
2		-2	
3		-3	
4		-4	
5		-5	
6		-6	
7		-7	

4   If two's complement notation is used, what connects the most significant bit (left hand bit) in the counter and the sign of the number it contains?

5   If two's complement notation is being used, what range of numbers is available?

6   Look carefully at columns two and four in the table above. If you look at (a) the last two digits, and (b) the last three digits in each column, can you see a connection? Can you see where the name "two's complement" comes from?

7   Can you find a way of working out the two's complement binary form of a negative integer directly from the binary form of the corresponding positive integer?

Investigating Shift Operations

Exercises 69 to 72 use the program *Shift* to explore various shift and rotate operations. This program can be downloaded from the publisher's website and should run on any computer running the Windows operating system.

The objective of Exercise 69 is to let students experiment with logical and arithmetic shift operations and see why the arithmetic shift is needed for division of negative numbers.

Exercise 70 gives further practice on arithmetic and logical shifts, highlighting the issue of overflow.

Exercise 71 lets students experiment with rotate operations, both with and without rotation through the carry bit.

Exercise 72 gives further practice with all four shift / rotate operations, using assembly language-style mnemonics.

Delivery

1. Decide whether you want students to work individually or in pairs. The latter encourages them to discuss their findings.

2. Get the students to load the program. Issue the operating instructions and either demonstrate the operation of the program centrally or give the students two or three minutes to try out the operating instructions.

3. Issue the appropriate exercise, then tour the room while the students work through their tasks.

4. When they have finished, hold a brief whole-class discussion to review the students' findings and to reinforce key points.

Timing

Allow 20 to 30 minutes for each activity.

Shift Operating Instructions

The program *Shift* simulates shift and rotate operations on an eight-bit register, including the use of the carry bit from the status register.

The program can be cycled through four modes using the *mode* button:

Logical shift

Arithmetic shift

Rotate with carry

Rotate without carry

- The *shift* buttons move the register contents to the left or right.

- Different starting values may be set up by clicking on individual digits.

The denary equivalent of the current register value is displayed in the bottom left corner.

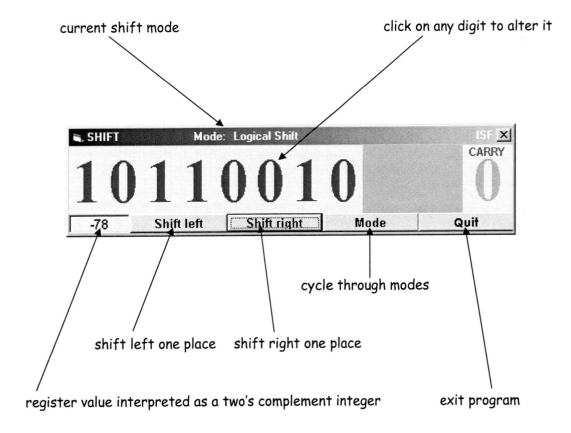

current shift mode

click on any digit to alter it

cycle through modes

shift left one place   shift right one place

register value interpreted as a two's complement integer   exit program

Exercise 69   Logical and Arithmetic Shifts

Load and run the program *Shift*, which simulates an eight bit register together with the carry bit from the processor's status register.   Check that the program is in logical shift mode.

Use the program to complete the tasks in the table, then answer the questions below.   The first task has been done for you.   Before each task, check that the contents of the register and the carry bit are correct.

| Task | Starting value | | Mode | Operation | Result | | |
	register	carry			binary	denary	carry
1	00011010 (26)	0	logical	shift right 1	00001101	13	0
2	00011010 (26)	0	logical	shift right 2			
3	00011010 (26)	0	logical	shift left 1			
4	00011010 (26)	0	logical	shift left 2			
5	11101011 (-21)	0	logical	shift left 1			
6	11101011 (-21)	0	logical	shift right 1			
7	00011010 (26)	0	arithmetic	shift right 1			
8	00011010 (26)	0	arithmetic	shift right 2			
9	00011010 (26)	0	arithmetic	shift left 1			
10	00011010 (26)	0	arithmetic	shift left 2			
11	11101011 (-21)	0	arithmetic	shift left 1			
12	11101011 (-21)	0	arithmetic	shift right 1			

Questions

1   What is the difference between arithmetic and logical shifts?

2   Which of the two types of shift works best for division?   Why?

3   What operation divides by 8?   Test your answer on 56, 32 and –8.

4   What operation multiplies by 16?   Test your answer on 2, 3 and –4.

5   How can a programmer tell when division by 2 gives a remainder?

6   Which of the above operations would you use to help test the value of bit 1 (the second from the right) in the register?

Exercise 70   Shifts and Overflow

Load and run the program *Shift*, which simulates an eight-bit register together with the carry bit from the processor's status register.

Use the program to complete the tasks in the table, then answer the questions below. The first task has been done for you. Before each task, check that the contents of the register and the carry bit are correct.

Task	Starting value		Mode	Operation	Result		
	register	carry			binary	denary	carry
1	00110010 (50)	0	logical	shift left 1	01100100	100	0
2	00011010 (50)	0	logical	shift left 2			
3	00011010 (50)	0	arithmetic	shift left 1			
4	00011010 (50)	0	arithmetic	shift left 2			
5	11011001 (-39)	0	logical	shift left 1			
6	11011001 (-39)	0	logical	shift left 2			
7	11011001 (-39)	0	arithmetic	shift left 1			
8	11011001 (-39)	0	arithmetic	shift left 2			
9	00111111 (63)	0	arithmetic	shift left 1			
10	11000010 (-62)	0	logical	shift left 1			

Questions

1   What is the largest positive number that can be doubled without overflow occurring?

2   What is the lowest negative number that can be doubled without overflow occurring?

3   What happens to the sign bit when a number is doubled using a logical shift and overflow occurs?

4   How can a programmer tell when multiplication by 2 results in overflow?

Exercise 71   Rotate Operations

Load and run the program *Shift*. Select the mode "rotate with carry".

Note that in this exercise we are not particularly concerned about denary values. They are included in the table below to help check your answers more readily.

1   Use the program to help you complete the following table:

Task	Starting value register	carry	Rotate Mode	Operation	Result binary	denary	carry
1	00100011 (35)	0	with carry	left 1			
2	00100011 (35)	0	with carry	right 1			
3	00100011 (35)	0	with carry	right 3			
4	00100011 (35)	0	with carry	right 8			
5	00100011 (35)	0	with carry	right 9			
6	00100011 (35)	1	without carry	left 1			
7	00100011 (35)	0	without carry	right 1			
8	00100011 (35)	0	without carry	right 3			
9	00100011 (35)	0	without carry	right 8			
10	00100011 (35)	0	without carry	right 9			

2   How is the carry bit used in the operation "rotate with carry"?

3   How is the carry bit used in the operation "rotate without carry"?

4   Set the mode to "rotate with carry". Using any starting value, carry out the following sequence of operations:

> rotate left 3
>
> change the carry bit
>
> rotate right 3

Record the result.

5   Set the mode to "rotate without carry". Using any starting value, carry out the same sequence of operations as in question 4 and record your result.

6   Based on the results of questions 4 and 5, can you think of a use for rotate operations?

86

Exercise 72   Further Shift Investigation

Load and run the program *Shift,* which simulates a processor register.

Assembly language instructions available to use with this register are:

RCR *n*   ;rotate right with carry *n* places

RCL *n*   ;rotate left with carry *n* places

ROR *n*   ;rotate right without carry *n* places

ROL *n*   ;rotate left without carry *n* places

SHR *n*   ;shift logical right *n* places

SHL *n*   ;shift logical left *n* places

SAR *n*   ;shift arithmetic right *n* places

SAL *n*   ;shift arithmetic left *n* places

CBS   ;set carry bit to 1

CBR   ;reset carry bit to 0

Use the program to answer the following questions:

1   Starting with the value 00110010 in the register and 0 in the carry bit each time, find the contents of the register and carry bit after each of the following operations:

    (i)   SAR 3

    (ii)   SHL 3

    (iii)   RCR 5

    (iv)   ROR 5

2   Starting with the value 11110010 in the register and 0 in the carry bit each time, find the contents of the register and carry bit after each of the following sequences of operations:

    (i)   SAR 2, SAL 2

    (ii)   RCL2, CBR, RCR 2

    (iii)   ROL 2, CBR, ROR 2

3   Suppose the eight bits in the register represent the states of eight actuators in a control system. Choose one of the three tasks below and carry it out, using only the operations listed above. When you have devised your solution, swap it with someone who has done a different task and test their solution using a range of different values.

A   Write down a sequence of instructions to reset bit 1 to zero and leave the rest of the register in its original state.

B   Write down a sequence of instructions to set bit 6 to one, again leaving the rest of the register in its original state.

C   Write down a sequence of instructions to set bits 0 to 2 to zero and leave the rest in their original state.

Answers

Exercise 1: Basic hardware components

A2, B3, C6, D1, E4, F5

Exercise 2: Application software

Most likely solution: A6, B5, C4, D3, E1, F2

There is some scope for discussion here. Some tasks, such as preparing the report, could be carried out using two or three of the applications, but the need to use every package exactly once is likely to lead to the above set of matches.

Exercise 3: Storage media

A5, B4, C6, D3, E2, F1

At the time of writing, memory sticks are evolving. They could be used for several of the tasks, but A5 currently seems the most likely and provides the best fit with the other media.

Exercise 4: Data representation 1 ('AS' Computing)

Most likely solution: A6, B4, C1, D2, E3, F5

A6 is better than D6 because arithmetic may need to be performed on exam marks. BCD is good for calculator displays because individual decimal digits are represented independently and can therefore be displayed and edited independently. Other choices settle themselves through the need to use each representation exactly once.

Exercise 5: Data representation 2 (A2 Computing)

Most likely solution: A4, B1, C5, D2, E6, F3

There is plenty of scope for discussion here. Telephone numbers require leading zeroes, so should not be stored as integers. In the case of the mobile phone display, digits must be stored independently. BCD and ASCII could be used for either version of the phone number; the former only uses 4 bits per digit, so saves space and is arguably more useful for the mobile phone.

Temperatures are more likely to be non-integer than student marks, so are more suited to floating point representation. The danger of rounding errors makes floating point unsuitable for amounts of money, which are usually stored in fixed point form or (in pence) as integers.

Exercise 6: Data validation

Most likely solutions: A3, B6, C1, D2, E4, F5 or A3, B6, C1, D2, E5, F4

There really is no one right set of answers here, so be prepared for an extended discussion. Product codes and account numbers *might* contain a check digit, but we know that ISBNs *definitely* do, which makes B6 a sensible choice. Picture checks might apply to product codes, depending on their exact format, and character counts to car registration numbers. Note that hash totals can be used only if data is batched before input.

Exercise 7: Data structures 1

A3&5, B1, C2&4

Ensure that each number has been used just once. It is worth emphasising that Task 3 involves (usually) a queue of characters, whereas Task 5 involves a queue of documents. Students sometimes fail to appreciate the difference.

Exercise 8: Data structures 2

A2, B4, C1, D5, E3

Infix and postfix notation are not included in every 'A' Level syllabus so may need explaining.

Exercise 9: HCI

A2, B1, C6, D4, E3, F5

Exercise 10: Systems development

A3, B6, C1, D5, E2, F4

There may be some need for discussion here, because terms can be used differently. For example, "implementation" is sometimes taken to include system development as well as installation, whereas here it is used to mean "installation".

Exercise 11: Legislation

A2, B1, C1, D2, E3, F3, G1, H2

Exercise 12: CPU components

A3, B4, C6, D2, E1, F5

A preliminary question and answer session on the abbreviations may be needed if students seem unsure about their meanings.

Exercise 13: Addressing modes

A4, B5, C2, D3, E1

Exercise 14: Operating system concepts

Most likely solution: A3, B5, C6, D1, E4, F2

There is some ambiguity surrounding the terms code sharing, access control and addressable blocks which could lead to fruitful discussion.

Exercise 15: Operating system terms

A4, B6, C1, D5, E2, F3

Exercise 16: Programming languages

Most likely solution: A6, B3, C5, D2, E4, F1

At a pinch most of these tasks *could* be done using most of the languages, so it is a matter of deciding the most suitable. This gives plenty of scope for discussion.

Exercise 17: LAN components

A6, B4, C5, D2, E1, F3

Exercise 18: Matching internet security methods

A5, B4, C2, D3, E6, F1

The answers may be well worth discussing with students, since the scope of such measures as passwords and encryption is often misunderstood.

Exercise 19: Internet services

A4, B6, C1, D3, E2, F5

This exercise provides an opportunity to stress that there is much more to the Internet than just the World Wide Web.

Exercise 20: Assembly language

A3, B1, C6, D4, E2, F5

While students may be used to different mnemonics from the ones employed here, they should be able to work out what these mean. The first instruction is intended more as a reminder of how -1 is stored in two's complement form than as an example of a useful instruction!

Exercise 21: Storage media

Task 1: Storage capacity, largest first

hard disk drive (typically 20 Gb+)

DVD-RW (typically 4.7 Gb)

CD (typically 700Mb)

RAM (typically 256 Mb)

memory stick (typically 64 Mb)

floppy disk (typically 1.44 Mb)

Task 2: Access time, fastest first

RAM

memory stick

hard disk drive

DVD-RW, CD-RW (dependent mainly on the drive speed)

floppy disk

Exercise 22: File organisation

The number of disk accesses, which take much longer than main memory accesses, is the critical factor. The phrase "several thousand customer records" is intended to indicate that only a small part of the file can be held in the disk buffer at any one time and therefore a large number of physical disk reads would be needed to access the whole file.

Task 1   Adding a record, fastest first.

Serial (record simply appended to the end)

Random Access (storage address calculated from primary key)

Indexed (store record in next available location, update index)

Sequential (re-write file, inserting record in correct place)

This, of course, is why serial organisation is normally used for transaction files.

Task 2   Retrieving a record, fastest first.

Random Access (storage address calculated from primary key)

Indexed (index in main memory searched to find storage address)

Sequential (records read in order until match found)

Serial   (records read in order until match found)

Accept an answer of "joint third" for the last two types. The sequential file is ranked higher only because if the record does not exist then searching can terminate sooner.

Note that, under some circumstances, collisions may make the random access file slower than a fully indexed one for both tasks, so allow this if students can justify it.

Exercise 23 – Exercise 26

These are dominoes games, so have no specific answers.

Exercise 27: Variables Bug Hunt 1

8 intended bugs:

Line 1	should read *Option Explicit*
Line 2	Missing *Sub*
Line 2	*Cluck* should be *Click*
Line 4	*Din* should be *Dim*
Line 5	*Total* should be defined as *Single*
Line 6	*,Text* should be *.Text*
Line 7	\ should be /
Line 8	*Vet* should be *Vat*

Exercise 28: Variable Bug Hunt 2

9 intended bugs:

Line 1	should read *Option Explicit*
Line 2	*Pirate* should read *Private*
Line 2	hyphen should be underscore
Lines 3,4	*Integer* should be *Single* (or *Double*) if <u>any</u> equation is to be solved
after Line 4	missing declaration *Dim x as Single* (or *Double*)
Lines 5,6	*.Txt* should read *.Text*
Lines 7,8	These lines are the wrong way round for a correct solution!
Line 9	The assignment should read *txtSolution.Text = x*
Line 10	*Sink Sub* should read *End Sub*

The program should be given to students **after** they have corrected it on paper, so that they can check their answers. Make sure they test it thoroughly, including decimal values, to show up the logical error in the original.

Exercise 29: Bug Hunt (For loop)

10 deliberate bugs

Line 2	*Loan* should be *Load*
Line 3	*Interger* should be *Integer*
Line 5	; should be , (or use separate *Dim* statement for *EndMiles*)
Line 7	should be *Form1.Show*
Line 9	*EndMales* should be *EndMiles*
Line 12	*From* should be =
Line 12	*By* should be *Step*
Line 13	Assignment is back to front
Line 14	*Kilometers* should be *Kilometres*
Line 15	*Loop* should be *Next* (or *Next Miles*)

Score: 7 errors good   10 errors excellent!

Exercise 30: Squares and Cubes Bug Hunt

10 known bugs:

Line 6	*Intiger* should be *Integer*
Line 9	*1* should be *0*
Line 11	Missing " before *Please*
Line 12	Should read *Value = Start*
Line 15	*Mid* should be *Mod*
Line 19	*Form1.Print.Value* should be *Form1.Print Value* (extra .)
Line 19	*Value + Value + Value* should be *Value * Value * Value*
Line 22	*Form1,Print* should be *Form1.Print*
Line 22	*ThreeCounties* should be *ThreeCount*
Line 23	*And* should be *End*

Score: 6 errors fair   8 good   10 excellent!

Exercise 31: Guessing Game Bug Hunt

12 known bugs:

Line 1	*Implicit* should be *Explicit*
Lines 2,3,5	*Is* should be *As* in each case (counted as one error)
Line 4	*Cluck* should be *Click*
Line 5	*Dum* should be *Dim*
Line 7	Assignment wrong way round
Line 11	> should read < (logical error)
Line 14	Missing " before *It*
Line 14	*Gos* should be *Goes*
Line 14/15	Missing End If
Line 19	Hyphen should be underscore
Line 21	*Valve* should be *Value*
Line 21	missing) after *100* [or after *1*]

Score: 7 errors fair   9 good   12 excellent!

Exercise 32   Procedure Bug Hunt

9 known bugs:

Line 4	The parameters *AByte* and *Even* are the wrong way round
Line 6	*Sob* should be *Sub*
Line 6	*ByVal* should be *ByRef* to allow the completed word to be returned
Line 6	*Is* should be *As*
Line 9	Duplicate declaration – this line must be removed
Line 14	*It* should be *If*
Line 15	*7* should be *8* (otherwise the lsb is not processed)
Line 19	*Pbit* should be *Position*
Line 20	*AByte* should be *Aword*

Score: 5 Fair 7 Good   9 Excellent

Exercise 33: Function Bug Hunt

10 known bugs:

Line 11	There should be no space between *Valid* and *Entry*
Line 11	the = sign should be *As*
Lines 11,12	missing *Dim OK As Boolean*
Line 12	*True* should be *False*
Line 13	*Or* should be *And*
Line 14	*AvScare* should be *AvScore*
Line 15	the first <= should be >=
Line 18	missing " " round message
Line 21	missing *If* after *End*
Line 30	should read *ValidEntry = OK*

Score: 5 Fair   7 Good   10 Excellent

Exercise 34: Array Bug Hunt

12 known bugs:

Line 2	*UpTo* should be *To*
Line 6	*String* should be *Integer*
Line 10	missing *For*
Line 11	*TotalPicked* should be *Position*
Line 12	*Fond* should be *Found*
Line 16	missing *Not* before *Found*
Line 17	*equals* should be =
Line 17/18	these lines should be swapped (or *+1* inserted in line 17 after *TotalPicked*)

Line 18/19	missing *End If*
Line 21	[ ] should be ( )
Line 22	missing " " round *Pele*
Line 23	*TotalPickled* should be *TotalPicked*

Score: 7 Fair   9 Good   12 Brilliant!

Exercise 35: Record Bug Hunt

10 known bugs (or 12 if the missing periods are counted separately):

Line 1	*Explisit* should be *Explicit*
Line 2	missing keyword *Private* at start of line
Line 5	*Sting* should be *String*
Line 9	*EmployeeRecord* should read *EmployeeRecordType* (or line 2 should be changed to match)
Line 10	there should be no space between *An* and *Employee*
Line 12/13/14	missing period before *Name*, *Job* and *DateEmployed*
Line 14	*DateEnployed* should be *DateEmployed*
Line 15	*EndWith* should be two separate words
Line 16	this line should come before *End With* (or have *AnEmployee* inserted before each fieldname)
Line 16	missing & before *.Name*

Score: 6 Fair   8 Good   10 Excellent

Exercise 36: File handling Bug Hunt 1

10 known bugs (all in display procedure):

Line 3	*Din* should be *Dim*
Line 6	Missing *Len = Len(Student)*
Line 7	*Len(1)* should be *LOF(1)*
Line 8	*0* should be *1* (or add *−1* to end of line)
Line 8	*NoOfRecord* should be *NoOfRecords*
Line 9	*Read* should be *Get*
Line 11	Missing . before *TG*
Line 11	*Age* should be *DoB*
After line 11	Missing *End With*
Line 13	*Shut* should be *Close*

Score: 6 Fair   8 Good   10 Excellent

Exercise 37: File Handling Bug Hunt 2

All 9 intentional bugs are in the delete procedure:

Line 7	*Rub* should be *Sub*
Line 11	*5* should be *6*
Line 15	*2* should be *1*
Line 18	= should be <>
Line 19	*Write* should be *Put*
Line 19	*1* should be *2*
After line 19	missing *End If*
Line 23	*Delete* should be *Kill*
Line 24	*Rename* should be *Name*

Score: 5 fair   7 good   9 excellent

Exercise 38: File Handling Bug Hunt 3

16 known bugs:

Line 1	should read *Option Explicit*
Line 2	*Typ* should be *Type*
Line 5	*Strong* should be *String*
Line 9	*6* should be *8* to match *IdNo* (*IdNo* could be changed to length *6* instead)
Line 10	*Dam Student* should be *Dim Student* (no comment!)
Line 12	Missing "
Line 16	*Sox* should read *Box*
Line 18	*Student* should be *Wanted*
Line 19	*Wanted* should be *Student*
Lines 20/27	Should have *Do* before *While* OR change *Loop* to *Wend*
Line 21	*#2* should be *#1*
Line 21	There should be a second comma before *Student*
Line 25	*TutorGroup* should be *TG*
Line 26	The assignment is the wrong way round
After line 26	Missing *End If*
Line 29	*Of* should be *If*

Score: 10 Good   12 Excellent   16 Brilliant

Exercise 39: Recursion Bug Hunt 1

The program should generate terms of the Fibonacci sequence 1,1,2,3,5,8,13 etc., displaying them in a listbox.

8 known errors:

line 5	*Cleer* should be *Clear*
line 8	*Add* should be *AddItem*
line 8	*Length* should be *Index*
line 11	missing *As* before final *Long*
line 12	*<* should be *<=*
line 15	*Term + 1* should be *Term – 1* and *Term + 2* should be *Term - 2*
line 15/16	missing *End If*
line 16	*Fun* should be *Function*

Score: 4 Fair   6 Good   8 Excellent

Exercise 40: Recursion Bug Hunt 2

The program should convert denary (decimal) numbers to binary. The form is shown after the number 83 has been processed.

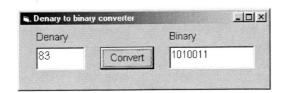

8 known errors:

line 2	*Pullic* should be *Public* (or *Private*)
line 2	*ByValue* should be *ByVal*
line 3	this line must come after the recursive call, i.e. after line 5
line 4	*0* should be *1* (to avoid leading zero in answer)
line 4	missing *Then*
line 5	*/* should be **
line 9	*Readabout* should be *Readout*

lines 9, 10   these lines must be reversed

Score: 4 fair   6 good   8 excellent

Exercise 41: Variable Bug Hunt

10 deliberate errors:

line 2	round brackets should be braces: {…}
line 3	missing semi-colon at end
line 5	*Began* should be *Begin*
line 6	missing apostrophe after *?*
line 9	missing brackets round *num1*
line 14	*number2* should be *num2*
line 17	missing semi-colon before = sign
line 18	missing comma after apostrophe and before *total*
line 19	*mean* should be *average*
line 20	missing full stop after *End*

Score: 6 fair   8 good   10 excellent

Exercise 42: Selection Bug Hunt

10 deliberate errors

line 3	= sign should be a colon
line 9	missing *Not* after *Or*
line 13	*Writ* should be *Write*
line 14	colon before = sign must be removed
line 14	apostrophes needed round *R*
line 15	semi-colon must be removed
line 17	missing (…) round '*pie*'
line 17	missing semi-colon (the only one needed after line 14!)
line 18	semi-colon must be removed
line 20	semi-colon must be removed

Score: 6 fair   8 good   10 excellent

Exercise 43 Loopy Bug Hunt

10 deliberate errors

line 1	missing comma between *Input* and *Output*
line 3	*Limit* should be added to list of integer variables
line 5	missing apostrophes around *How many rows?*
line 6	*Readin* should be *ReadIn*
line 10	semi-colon must be removed
line 12	*Far* should be *For*
line 12	semi-colon must be removed
line 13	first semi-colon should be colon
line 14/15	missing *End;* statement between lines 14 and 15
line 18	missing full stop

Score: 6 fair   8 good   10 excellent

Exercise 44: Procedures Bug Hunt

9 deliberate errors:

line 1	missing semi-colon at end
line 3	the first semi-colon should be a comma
line 5	*ch-count* should be *ch_count*
line 5	*1* should be *0* (or else a *–1* should be inserted in line 9)
line 6	*a_line* should be *line*
line 6	missing *Do*
line 7	semi-colon after *Then* must be removed
line 9	*Wroteln* should be *Writeln*
line 10	missing semi-colon at end

Score: 6 fair   8 good   9 excellent

Exercise 45 Array Bug Hunt

10 deliberate errors

line 3	(…) should be […]
line 3	*As* should be *Of*
line 4	= sign should be colon
line 4/5	missing *Begin* before line 5
line 7	colon should be semi-colon
line 8	*n* should be *index*
line 9	missing semi-colon
line 14	missing *[index]*
line 19	*To* should be *Downto*
line 23	*Readin* should be *Readln*

Score: 6 fair   8 good   10 excellent

Exercise 46: File Bug Hunt

12 deliberate errors

Note: it is assumed that the horizontal spacing of output is correct.

line 3	*Tipe* should be *Type*
line 6	colon should be = sign
line 9	*colors* should be *colours*
line 10	full stop should be semi-colon
line 11	*cars* should be *car*
line 15	*Rest* should be *Reset*
line 18	missing *Not* before *Eof*
line 19	*Start* should be *Begin*
line 20	missing comma after *carinfo*
line 21	*car* should be *vehicle*
line 22	*door* should be *doors*
lines 24/25	*Close(carinfo)* needed somewhere after line 24

Score: 7 fair   9 good   12 excellent

Exercise 47: Visual Basic Spot the Difference

```
1.        Dim Score(1 To 10) Is Integer          (1) Is should be As
2.        Dim N As Integer

3.        Private Sub Command1_Click()
4.        Text1.Text = Av(Score)                  (2) missing  , N
5.        End Sub

6.        Private Sub Form_Lead()                 (3) Lead should be Load
7.        Score(1) = 34
8.        Score(2) = 36
9.        Score(3) = 17
10.       Score(4) = 50
11.       Scorn(5) = 14                           (4) Scorn should be Score
12.       N = 5
13.       And Sub                                 (5) And should be End

14.       Public Function Av(ByRef Data, c As Integer) As Single

15.                                               (6) line missing
16.       Dum Total As Integer                    (7) Dum should be Dim
17.       For i = 1 To c
18.       Total + Score(i) = Total                (8) assignment reversed
                                                  (9) Score should be Data
                                                  (10) missing Next

19.       Av = Total / c
20.       End Function
```

Exercise 48: Pascal Spot the Difference (1)

```
1.     PROCEDURE analyse(number : LONGLNT);       (1) L should be I
2.     VAR divisor : LONGINT;                     (2) missing limit
3.          prime : BOOLEAN;
4.     BEGIN
5.     prime := true;
6.     limit := trunc(sqrt(number) -1);           (3) - should be +
7.     divisor := 1;
8.     REPEAT;                                     (4) unwanted semi-colon
9.         divisor = divisor + 1;                  (5) missing colon
10.       IF number MOD divisor := 0 THEN          (6) unwanted colon
11.           prim := false;                       (7) prim should be prime
12.    UNTIL (NOT prime) OR (divisor <= limit);    (8) < should be >
13.    WRITE (number, ' is ')                      (9) missing semi-colon
14.    IF prime AND (number = 2) THEN;             (10) AND --> OR, (11) unwanted semi-colon
15.        WRITELN (PRIME)                         (12) string should be in '    '
16.    ELSE                                        (13) missing line
17.    END {of analyse};
```

Exercise 49: Pascal Spot the Difference 2

Task 1

The program asks for a letter. If any of the capital letters N, E, W, S is entered, the corresponding compass direction is displayed and the program asks for another letter. This continues until a character that is not in the list is entered; at this the program ends.

Task 2 Find and correct eight deliberate errors:

```
1.      Program flight (Input, Output)            (1) missing semi-colon
2.      Var direction : Char;

3.      Begin
4.      Write ('Enter a letter ');
5.      Reedln (direction);                        (2) Reedln should be Readln
6.      While direction In ['U','D','S'] Do;       (3) semi-colon must be removed
7.         Begin
8.            Case direction Of
9.            'U' : Writeln(Up);                    (4) missing apostrophes round Up
10.           'D' : Writeln('Down');
11.           'S' : Writeln('Steady')
12.           End                                   (5) missing semi-colon
13.        Write (Enter a letter ');                (6) missing apostrophe before Enter
14.        Readln (letter)                          (7) letter should be direction
15.        End
16.     End                                         (8) missing full stop
```

Exercise 50: Java Spot the Difference

Task 1

The program asks the user to enter a positive integer, waits for them to do so, and checks that the integer is positive before outputting its square.

If the value is not positive, the message "You must enter a positive value" is displayed and the prompt "Enter a positive integer" is displayed on the next line. The program again waits for the user to enter a new value. This process is repeated until a positive value is entered.

Task 2 Correct the errors in the following similar program:

```
1.   System.out.print ("Enter a negative integer :    );        (1) missing quotes
2.   int value = Input.readInt();
3.   while (value >= 0);                                          (2) surplus semi-colon
4.   }                                                            (3) brace wrong way round
5.       System.out.println ("You must enter a negative value")
6.       value = Input.println();                                (4) should be readInt, and
                                                                      should be after next line
7.   System.out.print ("Enter a negative integer : ")           (5) missing semi-colon
8.   {                                                            (6) brace wrong way round
9.   System.out.println ("The square of your number is " &  value * value) );
                                                                 (7) & should be +
                                                                 (8) missing ( before value * value
```

Exercise 51: C Spot the Difference 1

Task 1

The program asks for two (floating point) numbers, checks for division by zero and outputs the result of dividing the first number by the second. It waits for a key to be pressed. If the letter "f" is pressed then the routine terminates, otherwise it repeats.

Task 2 Find and correct the eight deliberate errors in the following similar program:

```
1.   do {
2.       printf("\nEnter two numbers: ")           (1) missing semi-colon
3.       scant("%f %f",&x,&y);                      (2) scant should be scanf
4.       if (y < x) then                            (3) < should be >
                                                    (4) no then
5.           difference = y - x;
6.       else; {                                    (5) extra semi-colon - see also (7)
7.       difference = x - y;
8.       printf("The absolute difference is \n",difference); (6) missing %f before \n
9.       }                         (7) either this pair of brackets should be omitted or the closing
                                        bracket placed before the previous line
10.      printf("Press any key to continue or 'e' to end\n");
11.  } while (getch() != 'f');                      (8) 'f' should be 'e' to match previous
                                                        instruction
```

Exercise 52: C Spot the Difference 2

Task 1

The program section displays a heading "Table generator", asks for a number a in the range 1 to 10, then displays a multiplication table for the numbers 1 to a. Finally, it displays the message "Press 'f' to finish" and waits for the "f" key to be pressed, repeating the message if a different key is pressed.

Note that "\n" denotes a new line and "%4d" is a formatting code to provide spacing between numbers on a row.

Task 2 Find and correct the eight deliberate errors:

```
1.   {
2.       int  a,c,j;
3.       printf("Table generator\n");
4.       printf("\n")                              (1) missing semi-colon
5.       printf("Enter a whole number between 1 and 10 ");
6.       scare("%d", &a);                           (2) scare should be scanf
7.       printf("    ");
8.       for(c = 1; c <= a; c++)
9.           printf("%4d", c);
10.      printf("/n");                              (3) /n should be \n
11.      for(c := 1; c <= a; c++)                   (4) colon must be removed
12.          {
13.          printf("%4d" c);                       (5) missing comma before c
14.          for (j = 1; j <=a; j - -)              (6) j - - should be j++
15.              printf("%4d", c-j);
16.          printf("\n");                          (7) missing }
17.      do
18.          printf("Press 'f' to finish\n");
19.      while (gotcha() != 'f');                   (8) gotcha should be getch
20.  }
```

Exercise 53: Introduction to Computing Crossword

1 V		2 P		3 A	S	C	4 I	I	
D		R	5 S				M		
6 U	N	I	C	O	D	E	A		
		N	U				G		
7 B	I	T		8 N	U	9 M	B	E	R
Y		E		D		E		S	
T		R				M			10 T
E		11 T		12 M	O	U	S	E	
		E			R				X
	13 B	I	N	A	R	Y		14 I	T

Exercise 54: 'AS' Revision Crossword

	1 W		2 T		3 S	T	A	C	K			
4 M	O	D	E	M		T				5 K		
	R		X			O		6 B	E			
	7 D	8 A	T	A		9 P	10 A	R	I	T	Y	
		S				S		T				
		S		11 B	A	T	C	H				
12 Q	B	E		A		I		13 R	14 A	M		
U	M	U		15 F	I	L	E		O			
E	16 B	C	D				C		D			
17 U	R	L		18 V	E	C	T	O	R			
E		E					R					
	19 T	R	E	E		20 E	B	C	D	I	C	

Exercise 55: Programming Languages Crossword

	1 J		2 L								
3 B	A	S	I	C							
	V		S		4 F						
	A		5 P	R	O	L	O	G			
					R						
		6 S	7 M	A	L	L	T	A	L	K	
			O			R					
		8 A	D	A		9 P	A	S	10 C	A	11 L
			U					N	O		O
		12 A	L	G	O	L			B		G
			A						O		O
			2			13 P	E	R	L		

Exercise 56: Database and System Development Crossword

		1 D	2 D	L		3 P		4 D	B	M	5 S		6 P
			F			H					T		R
7 C	O	8 D	D			A		9 P	S	E	U	D	O
		I				S					D		T
		R				10 E	N	T	I	T	Y		O
11 B	E	T	12 A			D							T
		C	T				13 O	R	D	E	R	B	Y
14 B	I	T	T										P
O						15 D	A	T	A	B	A	S	E
Y	16 H	C	I			E							
C			B			17 S	E	L	E	18 C	T		
E			U			I				L		19 A	
	20 I	N	T	E	G	R	A	T	I	O	N		
			E			N					D		

Exercise 57: Processor and Low Level Programming Crossword

¹B	²R	A	N	C	H	▓	³D	▓	⁴P
▓	O	▓	▓	▓	⁵C	I	S	C	▓
⁶S	T	O	⁷R	E	▓	▓	R	▓	▓
▓	A	▓	E	▓	▓	▓	E	▓	▓
▓	T	▓	⁸L	O	G	I	C	A	⁹L
▓	E	▓	A	▓	▓	▓	T	▓	O
▓	▓	▓	T	¹⁰F	▓	▓	▓	▓	A
¹¹I	¹²N	D	I	R	E	¹³C	T	▓	D
▓	O	▓	V	▓	▓	I	▓	▓	▓
▓	T	▓	E	▓	¹⁴R	I	S	C	▓

Exercise 58: Binary Number Puzzle 1

¹1	0	²2	4	▓	▓	³1	⁴1	0	1
0	▓	3	⁵5	6	▓	1	▓	▓	▓
⁶1	0	0	⁷1	0	⁸7	0	▓	⁹1	
0	▓	▓	1	¹⁰1	5	▓	¹¹3	1	
0	¹²1	▓	¹³2	3	▓	¹⁴9	▓	1	
0	9	¹⁵1	0	¹⁶1	1	▓	1		
¹⁷1	0	¹⁸8	6	▓	1	▓	1		
0	¹⁹6	4	▓	²⁰1	1	²¹1	0	1	
▓	1	²²9	7	▓	8	▓	1		
²³1	0	2	4	▓	²⁴1	0	0	1	

Exercise 59: A2 Computing Binary Number Puzzle

¹1	•	²1	1	▓	▓	³1	⁴1	0	1
0	▓	•	⁵4	4	▓	2	▓	▓	
⁶1	0	1	⁷1	0	▓	⁸7	2	▓	⁹1
0	▓	▓	1	¹⁰1	8	▓	¹¹7	1	
0	¹²1	0	¹³1	0	▓	¹⁴4	▓	1	
0	▓	1	¹⁵1	1	¹⁶1	1	▓	1	
¹⁷1	0	¹⁸1	1	▓	0	▓	1		
0	¹⁹-	9	▓	²⁰1	1	²¹1	0	1	
▓	7	²²5	0	▓	8	▓	1		
²³-	1	1	3	▓	²⁴1	0	•	1	

Exercise 60: Hexadecimal Number Puzzle

¹1	0	²1	1	³1	0	⁴1	0
0	▓	A	▓	F	▓	8	▓
0	▓	⁵E	▓	⁶5	▓	⁷9	
⁸1	1	⁹1	0	¹⁰1	0	¹¹1	1
0	▓	D	▓	0	▓	E	▓
1	▓	¹²B	¹³A	C	▓	¹⁴A	¹⁵B
0	▓	7	▓	¹⁶8	▓	0	
¹⁷1	1	0	1	0	0	1	0

Exercises 61–64

These are Quick Quizzes. Answers are given in the text.

Exercises 65–67

These activities have no specific answers.

Exercise 68: Binary Investigation

1   When the counter passes 11111111 it goes to zero and starts again.

When it passes zero, going backwards, it goes to 11111111.

2    $2^8 = 256$ different numbers.   The range is 0 to 255.

3

denary	8-bit binary	denary	8-bit binary
0	00000000	0	00000000
1	00000001	-1	11111111
2	00000010	-2	11111110
3	00000011	-3	11111101
4	00000100	-4	11111100
5	00000101	-5	11111011
6	00000110	-6	11111010
7	00000111	-7	11111001

4   MSB = 0 for positive numbers. MSB = 1 for negative numbers.

This question may provoke some discussion of where the boundary between positive and negative numbers should be drawn. Note that we must take 10000000 to represent the number –128 for the rule to work.

5   –128 to +127. This should follow readily from Question 4.

6   The sum of the last two digits from n and –n is always 4 (2^2).

The sum of the last three digits from n and –n is always 8 (2^3).

[In general, the sum of the last m digits is always 2^m.]

So taking a positive number from a power of two gives the corresponding negative value. Hence the name "two's complement."

7   There is plenty of scope for discussion here. Students may well base their answer directly on question 6 if they have thought that one through fully. They can also be shown the method that many students find easiest in practice:

"Starting from the right:

- leave all digits up to and including the first "1" alone.

- Invert all other digits."

Exercise 69

Task	Result		
	binary	denary	carry
1	00001101	13	0
2	00000110	6	1
3	00110100	52	0
4	01101000	104	0
5	11010110	-42	1
6	01110101	117	1
7	00001101	13	0
8	00000110	6	1
9	00110100	52	0
10	01101000	104	0
11	11010110	-42	1
12	11110101	-11	1

1   A logical shift moves all bits in the register, whereas an arithmetic shift preserves the sign bit.

A logical right shift always inserts a zero in the MSB, whereas an arithmetic right shift copies the sign bit to the bit on its right.

2   Arithmetic, because negative integers can be divided correctly.

3   Arithmetic right shift 3 places.

4   Arithmetic or logical shift left 4 places.

5   By testing the carry bit to see if it is equal to 1.

6   Arithmetic or logical right shift 2 places.

Exercise 70

Task	Result		
	binary	denary	carry
1	01100100	100	0
2	11001000	-56	0
3	01100100	100	0
4	01001000	72	1
5	10110010	-78	1
6	01100100	100	1
7	10110010	-78	1
8	11100100	-28	0
9	01111110	126	0
10	10000100	-124	1

1   63

2   -64

3   The sign bit changes.

4   This can lead to involved discussion of how to test for the sign bit changing.

Note that not all processors include an arithmetic left shift in their instruction set.

Exercise 71

1

Task	Result		
	binary	denary	carry
1	01000110	70	0
2	00010001	17	1
3	11000100	-60	0
4	01000110	70	0
5	00100011	35	0
6	01000110	70	0
7	10010001	-111	1
8	01100100	100	0
9	00100011	35	0
10	10010001	-111	1

2   It moves around with the other bits.

3   It is not rotated, but records the last bit to be shifted off the end of the register.

4   Bit 5 is altered.

5   Nothing is altered.

6   For example, rotate with carry could be used with a sequence similar to that in Question 4 as an alternative to a logic operation to change one bit in a register.

   Rotate without carry could be used with a sequence such as that in Question 5 to test a bit and return the register to its original state.

Possible follow-up question: "Can you give some pairs of rotate operations that are equivalent?" (E.g. ROL 3, ROR 5)

Exercise 72

1   (i)   00000110 0
     (ii)   10010000 1
     (iii) 00100001 1
     (iv)   10010001 1

2   (i)   11110000 1
     (ii)   10110010 0
     (iii) 11110010 1

3   Possible solutions:
     A   RCR 2
          CBR
          RCL 2
     B   RCL 2
          CBS
          RCR 2
     C   RCR 1
          CBR
          RCR 1
          CBR
          RCR 1
          CBR
          RCL 3

Index